Contemporary's Whole Language Series

VIEWPOINTS

NONFICTION SELECTIONS

Cathy Niemet
Project Editor

Karen A. Fox
Research and Development

CONTEMPORARY BOOKS

a division of NTC/CONTEMPORARY PUBLISHING GROUP
Lincolnwood, Illinois USA

Photo Credits: p. 2—AP/Wide World Photos; p. 18—© Bob
Daemmrich/Stock, Boston; p. 36—© Robert F. Rodriguez;
p. 54—The Bettmann Archive; p. 72—© Deborah Kahn
Kalas/Stock, Boston; p. 86—AP/Wide World Photos; p. 98—
© Craig Aurness/West Light; p. 110—The Bettmann
Archive.

Viewpoints 1 : nonfiction selections.
     p.   cm.
    ISBN 0-8092-3992-2 (paper)
    1. Readers for new literates.
PE1126.A4V54   1991
428.6′2.—dc20   91-30924
                   CIP

0 1 2 3 4 5 6 7 QB(M) 23 22 21 20 19 18 17 16 15 14 13
ISBN: 0-8092-3992-2

Published by Contemporary Books,
a division of NTC/Contemporary Publishing Group, Inc.,
4255 West Touhy Avenue,
Lincolnwood (Chicago), Illinois 60712-1975 U.S.A.
© 1992 by NTC/Contemporary Publishing Group, Inc.

Editorial Director Caren Van Slyke	*Production Editor* Marina Micari
Assistant Editorial Director Mark Boone	*Cover Design* Georgene Sainati
Editorial Lisa Black Craig Bolt Janet Fenn Esther Johns Leah Mayes Erica Pochis	*Cover Illustrator* Maria Stroster *Art & Production* Carolyn Hopp *Typography* Terrence Alan Stone
Editorial Production Manager Norma Fioretti	

TO THE READER

What will you find in this book? Readable, interesting selections chosen with you in mind.

As you read, you will meet a singer and guitarist who won a Grammy Award at age 92, a homeless man who sneaked into someone's home to cook a meal, and Nolan Ryan, who as a young boy knew that he would one day become a famous major-league baseball pitcher. You will read about a Mexican-Chinese woman and an African-American woman who have broken ground in nontraditional jobs, an Indian chief's farewell address to his people, a Japanese woman's memories of her experiences in a prison camp, and a humble, self-taught scholar who lives in the backwoods of Arkansas.

Like you, the people have experienced great moments, loving families, and pride in work well done. They have laughed, realized dreams, written letters to loved ones, and thought about the meaning of home.

After you read each selection, take time out to reflect and to write. Draw on your own experiences to understand the experiences of the people you read about. On your way to understanding them, you will come to understand more about yourself.

We hope that you enjoy *Viewpoints.*

The Editors

CONTENTS

Elizabeth Cotten at age 92 holding the Grammy award she received for best traditional folk recording in 1984

GREAT MOMENTS

Have you ever felt defeated and that everything and everyone was against you? Have you felt you could be happier if there weren't so many roadblocks between you and a goal?

Many people must overcome great roadblocks in their lives. Some people have mental or physical disabilities. Others suffer from poverty or discrimination.

The following readings are about people who overcame barriers. Their lives and stories are different. But they were all looking for ways to express themselves. The "odds were against them," but they overcame the barriers. Each lived a full life. As you read, think about what roadblock each person had to overcome in order to achieve success.

Elizabeth (Libba) Cotten was born in January 1892 in Chapel Hill, North Carolina. She died on June 29, 1987, in Syracuse, New York. She won a Grammy award in 1984 for her music on "Elizabeth Cotten Live!"

Libba Cotten was a singer, storyteller, composer, guitarist, and banjo player. She worked as a housekeeper for years before beginning a performing career at age sixty-seven. She is the author of many songs, including the folk music classic, "Freight Train." The song has been recorded by groups as diverse as Peter, Paul, and Mary and the Grateful Dead. Until her death at age ninety-five, Elizabeth Cotten continued to perform around the country. She invented the three-fingered style of guitar picking that is now called "Cotten pickin'."

Elizabeth Cotten

From *I Dream a World*
Brian Lanker

I named myself. The first day I went to school, the teacher was calling roll and everybody was called a name. My parents didn't name me. They all called me Sis, you know. So when the teacher got to me, she said, "Li'l Sis, don't you have a name? What is it?" And I just said, "Elizabeth." I don't know where I got that name. So she put it down and I started being called Elizabeth.

When I was a little girl my mother and father used to bury their meat. Rub it up and bury it in the ground and put dirt back over it like we didn't have no meat. The white people would come and take it away from us. My mother said she could hear the horses' feet coming over the bridge. And she said, "Neville, you better go hidin' it." She'd tell him, "Hide the meat, I hear the horses' feet." He'd leave a bone where he done cut all the meat off and leave that in the meat house like the meat gone. And then he'd dig a hole and put all the meat in it. They'd come around and look for it. If he didn't hide some of it he wouldn't have none when they left.

When I was a child I went to the door and asked people if they needed somebody to work. I said, "I can wash your dishes, I can set your table, and I can sweep your kitchen and everything." And I went to work for this lady for seventy-five cents a month.

I saved my money and gave it to my mother and when she got enough we bought a guitar. I carried it home and started pluckin' on it. My mother said, "Now if you don't put that thing down, I'm gonna git ya. I gotta get to sleep and to work in the mornin'." And I'd say, "Mama, I'm gonna stop. This is the last song." And I just keep everybody awake all night. Lord have mercy. I was a nuisance, I know I was. But my mama would always say, "She's my baby. Now let her do what she wants to do. She ain't doin' nothin' wrong."

I didn't have no lessons. Not nobody teach me. I didn't know nothin'. I worked hard. I started playin' one string at a time. Get a song and get a string and just play up and down. And then I tried to play more strings into the song.

All my brothers could play. Sometimes I'd ask my brothers to show me how to make a chord on the guitar. They said, "I can't show you how to do it. You got your fingers on the wrong strings. You're playin' the left hand and you never stop pickin'. Change the strings and put your fingers on like I tell ya." I couldn't do it. I was playin' my guitar left-handed and I didn't change the strings.

I pick the tune, you know, just on the strings. That's the way I did all my songs. I reckon that's why they named it "Cotten pickin'."

I went to work for the Seeger family [which included folk singers Mike and Pete Seeger]. I did everything, cooked, washed dishes, served. One day, Michael says to me, "Elizabeth, why don't we give a little concert?" They knew I could play because I was playin' the guitar ever' minute I got. We had that concert and I stopped work then and went on out to play.

Say I'm a musician if you want to, but I didn't know one chord from another. I don't know it yet, I mean in letters. Just let me pick and sing.

I just love to sing. I love to get up before people and let 'em hear what I can do. It does me good to play my guitar. I love to entertain people, sing to 'em, talk, tell little things about me, what all I used to do. That was my pleasure to do that.

I was just glad to get the Grammy. I didn't know what the thing was. It's the honor what I loved.

When Helen Keller was two years old, a serious illness destroyed her sight and hearing. Unable to see, hear, or speak, she was cut off from her world. Anne Sullivan, a teacher, came to live with the Kellers when Helen was seven. Miss Sullivan's relationship with Helen and the story of how Helen learned to communicate is told in the play and film, The Miracle Worker.

This reading is from a biography, The Helen Keller Story. *It describes the "miracle" that opened Helen's world.*

Miracle at the Pump House

From *The Helen Keller Story*
Catherine Owens Peare

Miss Sullivan took her by the hand and they went for a carriage drive. When the carriage stopped, they alighted[1] and entered a different house. Helen groped her way about the room, recognizing nothing, until her companion placed one of her own dolls in her arms. She clung to the familiar thing. But as soon as Helen realized that she was alone with the stranger in a strange place, that no amount of rubbing her cheek would bring her mother, she flung the doll away in a rage. She refused to eat, refused to wash, and gave the governess[2] a long, violent tussle when it came time to go to bed.

---

[1]came down
[2]a woman employed in a private home to train and teach children

The governess did not seem very tall, but she was strong and stubborn, and for the first time in her life Helen began to experience defeat. She grew tired, wanted to lie down and sleep, but still she struggled against the stranger's will. She would sleep on the floor, or in the chair! But each time she was dragged back to the bed. At last Helen felt herself giving in, and, exhausted by her own efforts, and huddled close to the farthest edge of the big double bed, she fell asleep.

When Helen awoke in the morning, she flung herself out of bed prepared to give further resistance, but somehow her face was washed with less effort than the night before, and after she had dressed and eaten her breakfast she felt her companion's determined but gentle hands guiding her fingers over some soft, coarse yarn, guiding them again along a thin bone shaft with a hooked end. In a very little while Helen had grasped the idea of crocheting, and as she became interested in making a chain she forgot to hate Anne Sullivan.

Each day in the new house after that brought new skills to be learned—cards to sew, beads to string.

After about two weeks, Helen had begun to accept her routine, her table manners, her tasks, her companion. The whole world seemed to grow gentler as her own raging disposition[3] subsided.[4]

She cocked her head suddenly one afternoon and sniffed the air, detecting a new odor in the room, something familiar—one of her father's dogs! Helen groped about until she found the silken, long-haired setter, Belle. Of all the dogs on the farm, Belle was Helen's favorite, and she quickly lifted one of Belle's paws and began to move the dog's toes in one of the

---

[3]temperament; frame of mind
[4]became less active

finger tricks. Miss Sullivan patted Helen's head, and the approval made her feel almost happy.

Miss Sullivan soon took her by the hand and led her out the door, across a yard, to some front steps, and instantly Helen realized where she was. She was home! She had been in the little annex[5] near home all this time. Mother and Father had not been far away. She raced up the steps and into the house and flung herself at one adult after another. She was home! Scrambling up the stairs to the second floor, she found her own room just the same, and when she felt Miss Sullivan standing behind her she turned impulsively and pointed a finger at her and then at her own palm. Who was she?

"T-e-a-c-h-e-r," Anne Sullivan spelled into her hand.

But the finger trick was too long to be learned at once.

Every day after that Teacher and Helen were constant companions indoors and out, and gradually Helen learned to see with her fingers. Teacher showed her how to explore plants and animals without damaging them—chickens, grasshoppers, rabbits, squirrels, frogs, wildflowers, butterflies, trees. Grasshoppers had smooth, clear wings; the wings of a butterfly were powdery. The bark of a tree had a curious odor, and through its huge trunk ran a gentle humming vibration.

Hand-in-hand they wandered for miles over the countryside, sometimes as far as the Tennessee River where the water rushed and churned over the mussel[6] shoals.[7]

---

[5]a wing or addition added on to a building
[6]small sea animals with shells
[7]where water is shallow and hard to navigate

For everything she felt or did there was a finger trick: wings, petals, river boats—walking, running, standing, drinking.

One morning when she was washing her face and hands, Helen pointed to the water in the basin, and Teacher spelled into her hand: "w-a-t-e-r." At the breakfast table later Helen pointed to her mug of milk, and Teacher spelled: "m-i-l-k." But Helen became confused. "D-r-i-n-k" was milk, she insisted. Helen pointed to her milk again and Teacher spelled, "m-u-g." Was m-u-g d-r-i-n-k? In another second Helen's mind was a jumble of wiggling fingers. She was frustrated, bewildered, angry, a bird trapped in a cage and beating her wings against the bars.

Quickly Teacher placed an empty mug in her hand and led her out-of-doors to a pump that stood under a shed in the yard. Helen stood before the pump, mug in hand, as Teacher indicated, and felt the rush of cold water over her hands. Teacher took one of her hands and spelled, "w-a-t-e-r." While water rushed over one hand Helen felt the letters, w-a-t-e-r, in the other.

Suddenly Helen was transfixed,[8] and she let her mug crash to the ground forgotten. A new, wonderful idea . . . back into her memory rushed that infant's word she had once spoken: "wah-wah." She grew excited, her pulse raced, as understanding lighted her mind. Wah-wah was w-a-t-e-r. It was a word! These finger tricks were words! There were words for everything. That was what Teacher was trying to tell her.

She felt Teacher rush to her and hug her, and Teacher was as excited as she, crying and laughing, because at last Helen understood the concept of words.

---

[8]made motionless

Joyfully they ran back into the house, and Helen was surrounded by an excited household. All the rest of the day she demanded words, words, words. What was this? What was that? Even the infant Mildred? What was that? "B-a-b-y." And once more Helen pointed a persistent finger at Miss Sullivan and demanded the word that would identify *her*.

"T-e-a-c-h-e-r," Anne Sullivan spelled. "T-e-a-c-h-e-r."

The last shred of hostility and hate vanished from Helen's soul as she glowed with her sudden happiness. She felt her fingers being lifted to Teacher's face to explore its expression. The corners of the mouth were drawn up and the cheeks were crinkled. Helen imitated the expression, and when she did her face was no longer blank, because Helen Keller was smiling.

When bedtime finally arrived, she put her hand willingly into Teacher's and mounted the stairs, and before climbing into bed she slipped her arms around Teacher's neck and kissed her—for the first time.

Christy Brown was born June 5, 1932, with cerebral palsy. At the time, people did not understand birth defects or disabilities. The doctors told Christy's parents that he was an "imbecile" and said he had little or no intelligence. Most children like Christy were put in special homes to be taken care of. Christy stayed with his family of fourteen because his mother believed that while his body was disabled, his mind was not.

Christy was unable to communicate by speaking. His upper body was paralyzed, so he could not use his hands to sign or write. At age five, something happened that changed Christy's life. This story is from his autobiography.

The Letter "A"

From *My Left Foot*
Christy Brown

I was now five, and still I showed no real sign of intelligence. I showed no apparent interest in things except with my toes—more especially those of my left foot. Although my natural habits were clean, I could not aid myself, but in this respect my father took care of me. I used to lie on my back all the time in the kitchen or, on bright warm days, out in the garden, a little bundle of crooked muscles and twisted nerves, surrounded by a family that loved me and hoped for me and that made me part of their own warmth and humanity. I was lonely, imprisoned in a world of my own, unable to communicate with others, cut off, separated from them as though a glass wall stood between my existence and theirs, thrusting me beyond the sphere of their lives and activities. I longed to run about and play with the rest, but I was unable to break loose from my bondage.[1]

Then, suddenly, it happened! In a moment everything was changed, my future life molded into a definite shape, my mother's faith in me rewarded and her secret fear changed into open triumph.

It happened so quickly, so simply after all the years of waiting and uncertainty, that I can see and feel the whole scene as if it had happened last week. It was the afternoon of a cold, gray December day. The streets outside glistened with snow, the white sparkling flakes stuck and melted on the windowpanes and hung on the boughs of the trees like molten silver. The wind howled dismally, whipping up little whirling columns of snow that rose and fell at every fresh gust. And over all, the dull, murky sky stretched like a dark canopy,[2] a vast infinity[3] of grayness.

Inside, all the family were gathered round the big kitchen fire that lit up the little room with a warm glow and made giant shadows dance on the walls and ceiling.

In a corner Mona and Paddy were sitting, huddled together, a few torn school primers before them. They were writing down little sums on to an old chipped slate, using a bright piece of yellow chalk. I was close to them, propped up by a few pillows against the wall, watching.

---

[1]physical restraint
[2]cover
[3]endless or unlimited space

It was the chalk that attracted me so much. It was a long, slender stick of vivid yellow. I had never seen anything like it before, and it showed up so well against the black surface of the slate that I was fascinated by it as much as if it had been a stick of gold.

Suddenly, I wanted desperately to do what my sister was doing. Then—without thinking or knowing exactly what I was doing, I reached out and took the stick of chalk out of my sister's hand—with my left foot.

I do not know why I used my left foot to do this. It is a puzzle to many people as well as to myself, for, although I had displayed a curious interest in my toes at an early age, I had never attempted before this to use either of my feet in any way. They could have been as useless to me as were my hands. That day, however, my left foot, apparently by its own volition,[4] reached out and very impolitely took the chalk out of my sister's hand.

I held it tightly between my toes, and, acting on an impulse, made a wild sort of scribble with it on the slate. Next moment I stopped, a bit dazed, surprised, looking down at the stick of yellow chalk stuck between my toes, not knowing what to do with it next, hardly knowing how it got there. Then I looked up and became aware that everyone had stopped talking and was staring at me silently. Nobody stirred. Mona, her black curls framing her chubby little face, stared at me with great big eyes and open mouth. Across the open hearth, his face lit by flames, sat my father, leaning forward, hands outspread on his knees, his shoulders tense. I felt the sweat break out on my forehead.

My mother came in from the pantry with a steaming pot in her hand. She stopped midway between the

---

[4]the will to do something

table and the fire, feeling the tension flowing through
the room. She followed their stare and saw me in the
corner. Her eyes looked from my face down to my
foot, with the chalk gripped between my toes. She put
down the pot.

Then she crossed over to me and knelt down
beside me, as she had done so many times before.

"I'll show you what to do with it, Chris," she said,
very slowly and in a queer, choked way, her face
flushed as if with some inner excitement.

Taking another piece of chalk from Mona, she
hesitated, then very deliberately drew, on the floor in
front of me, *the single letter "A."*

"Copy that," she said, looking steadily at me.
"Copy it, Christy."

I couldn't.

I looked about me, looked around at the faces that
were turned towards me, tense, excited faces that were
at that moment frozen, immobile, eager, waiting for a
miracle in their midst.

The stillness was profound.[5] The room was full of
flame and shadow that danced before my eyes and
lulled my taut[6] nerves into a sort of waking sleep. I
could hear the sound of the water tap dripping in the
pantry, the loud ticking of the clock on the mantel-
shelf, and the soft hiss and crackle of the logs on the
open hearth.

I tried again. I put out my foot and made a wild
jerking stab with the chalk, which produced a very
crooked line and nothing more. Mother held the slate
steady for me.

"Try again, Chris," she whispered in my ear.
"Again."

---

[5]intense
[6]tightly stretched

I did. I stiffened my body and put my left foot out again, for the third time. I drew one side of the letter. I drew half the other side. Then the stick of chalk broke and I was left with a stump. I wanted to fling it away and give up. Then I felt my mother's hand on my shoulder. I tried once more. Out went my foot. I shook, I sweated and strained every muscle. My hands were so tightly clenched that my fingernails bit into the flesh. I set my teeth so hard that I nearly pierced my lower lip. Everything in the room swam till the faces around me were mere patches of white. But—I drew it—*the letter "A."* There it was on the floor before me. Shaky, with awkward, wobbly sides and a very uneven center line. But it *was* the letter "A." I looked up. I saw my mother's face for a moment, tears on her cheeks. Then my father stooped and hoisted me on to his shoulder.

I had done it! It had started—the thing that was to give my mind its chance of expressing itself. True, I couldn't speak with my lips. But now I would speak through something more lasting than spoken words— written words.

That one letter, scrawled on the floor with a broken bit of yellow chalk gripped between my toes, was my road to a new world, my key to mental freedom. It was to provide a source of relaxation to the tense, taut thing that was I, which panted for expression behind a twisted mouth.

REFLECT······································

What roadblock did Elizabeth Cotten, Helen Keller, and Christy Brown each overcome? How did each person's life change as a result of overcoming the roadblock?

Which two people's stories are similar? Why?

Explain how all three people shared the same goal of wanting to communicate with others.

Each of the three people had the support of another person. Tell who helped each one.

Which details show that Elizabeth Cotten's childhood was disadvantaged?

WRITE·······································

Is there a roadblock that is stopping you from reaching one of your goals? Write a paragraph describing how you might overcome the roadblock.

Which of the three people in the readings do you most admire? Why? Write a letter to the person explaining your views.

Do you know someone who has had a "great moment" like the ones these three people experienced? Describe the person and what happened because of that moment.

A Hispanic family standing proudly in front of their home in Texas

FAMILY RELATIONSHIPS

As a child, were you raised in a traditional family, with a mother, father, brothers, and sisters? Or were you raised by a stepmother, a grandparent, an aunt, or someone not a blood relative?

Regardless of how people are related, families come in all shapes and sizes. Each family has its own unique personal, cultural, and religious beliefs and customs. Most families feel love. Some families show love better than others. All three readings focus on loving family relationships.

As you read, think about your relationships with the members of your family.

This true story won an award for "Best Feature Story for Sports." But there is not much in this reading about football or sports. Instead, we learn about the love between two men who put each other first in their lives.

The son is young and at the beginning of his pro football career. His stepfather is dying. Together, they add a whole new meaning to the sportsmanship rule "the most important thing in life is not winning, but how you play the game."

Mark Messner

From *Detroit Free Press*
Mitch Albom

Isn't life funny, Mark Messner thought. He held a spoonful of malted shake up to his father's lips, which were black and peeling, burned from chemotherapy.[1] "Here you go, Dad," he said. His father rolled his eyes and made a "mmm" sound, like a child. Mark smiled, pulled the spoon out and dug it back into the cup.

Isn't life funny? A few weeks ago, Messner, 22, was a rookie linebacker for the Los Angeles Rams. He was getting paid to play football. He was living in sunny southern California. Then the phone rang. "You'd better come home," his sister said. He knew what that meant. He left the team, without pay, and boarded a plane for Detroit.

---

[1] the treatment of cancer with drugs

When he first saw his father, lying in the hospital bed, Mark bit his lip. Then he went out in the hall and began to sob. He showed the nurse an old photo, before the disease, and she said, "Oh, my God."

Now he sat by the bed and fed his father, the way Del Pretty had done for him when he was an infant. Of course, technically, Del was his stepfather, but Mark never cared for that phrase. He figured if the man raised me, fed me, spanked me, hugged me, took me to school, wrote me poems, came to all my football games and made me feel like the most important person in the world, well, the hell with it. He is my father.

And I am his son.

"Have some more, Dad," he whispered. He looked at the blotches of red along Del's arms and legs. He saw the blood stains on the sheets where the skin had peeled away. He thought back to a year ago, when life seemed so carefree. He was heading to the Rose Bowl with the Michigan Wolverines. There would be Hawaii after that and Japan after that. And then came the NFL draft. The Rams took him with a low-round pick. Then in training camp they had him carrying the red cones up and down the field, like some equipment boy.

"Dad," Mark said one night in a phone call home. "You'd better pull my resume off my computer. I can't compete on this level."

"Just keep plugging," Del said.

"But they got me *moving cones!*"

"They didn't draft you to move cones."

What does he know? Mark thought. He's never been in the NFL. He owns a piano store, for Pete's sake. But eventually the Rams did come around. He stopped moving cones. He played in the exhibition games. He made the team. His father had been right. Again.

Mark looked at him. The room was quiet. He dug the spoon into the melting chocolate.

*   *   *

Take the chemo, they had told him.

"No," he had said.

"There's no alternative."

"There's got to be an alternative."

Del Pretty had been diagnosed as having lymph node cancer in 1980. He fought the very idea, as if it had somehow insulted his pride. He scorned chemotherapy, because he felt it would deteriorate[2] him. Instead he searched for other methods. He tried special diets and experimental drugs. And eventually he beat the illness into remission.[3] Who had time to be sick? There was the business. The family. And Mark's football games.

"He never missed one," Mark recalls. "He came to all the home games at Michigan and a lot of the road ones, too. There was this game in Indiana where the weather was horrible. He sat there in the rain the whole time."

Not that he was one of those jock-hungry fathers. On the contrary, Del Pretty was *not* a very athletic man. Silver-haired, dapper,[4] with glasses and a gentle but disciplined expression, he looked more like a well-placed accountant. Which he was. But he loved his children. He would show his feelings quietly, in notes that Mark found in his college mailbox: *"Dear Mark, I want you to know how proud you make me feel."*

Mark's friends would tease him sometimes about how close he was with Del. It was almost corny. He had chosen Michigan over UCLA because he wanted Del to be able to see him play. Before he left for the

---

[2] to make or become worse
[3] lessening or disappearance of the symptoms of a disease
[4] trim, neat, or smart in dress or appearance

Rams, Mark gave his Dad a record. "Wind Beneath My Wings" by Bette Midler. He told him to listen to the words, because that's how he felt. *"Did I ever tell you you're my hero. You're everything I wish I could be."*

It was the stuff of sappy movies. Unless you know the whole story. Mark was the son of divorce. Several times, his mother married and remarried. His natural father (Max Messner, a former NFL player) also remarried. The one constant in his life was Del. He was there when Mark had problems. He was there when Mark wanted to talk about life, or girls, or football. He gave honest answers. Strict, but from the heart.

When Del and Mark's mother divorced, it tore Mark apart. His Dad had to live alone in some apartment in Northville. Why? It's not fair.

And then the cancer came back.

*   *   *

Take the chemo, they told him.

"No," he said.

Once again he tried experimental drugs. He flew to Houston for a new pill. He flew to California for a procedure in which animals are injected with samples from the patient's tumors, then the antibodies formed are injected into the patient.

"I'm sorry," the doctor said. "The process takes six to eight months."

"Yes?" said Del.

"Well, quite frankly, I don't think you have that long."

What do you do when a doctor tells you that? Already the disease had changed him physically. The tumors were stealing nutrients from his food and releasing lymph fluid instead into his abdomen. He was bloated like a pregnant woman.

"He couldn't sleep in a bed anymore," says Messner. "His stomach was so large. But meanwhile, the rest of his body was suffering from malnutrition."

Alone, out of options, he went to doctors in Ann Arbor. "Chemotherapy," they said. It was early fall. Football season. Mark was in L.A., getting paid. It was as if Del had held out all this time, just to make sure his son could handle adulthood.

"All right," Del said, finally. "I'll try the chemotherapy."

They put the needle in his arm.

*   *   *

The blotches began after the second treatment. They looked like a rash. He asked his doctors. "Must be a skin condition," they said. "Have you changed your soap recently?"

His soap?

Another round of chemo, an increased dosage. Now the skin began to pus and fester. Like a horrible sunburn, it would die and peel away. His back. His legs. Around his mouth. Without so much as a match's flame, he was burnt all over.

"It was the chemo," says Mark now. "And what was happening outside was happening inside him as well. The organs were being destroyed." How could this be? Wasn't chemo supposed to help him? You would touch his back and the skin would come off in your hands. One time, a nurse tried rubbing ointment on the sores. Del began to moan in pain. Mark came running in.

"What's wrong, what's he saying?" the nurse asked.

"He's saying don't rub, don't rub," said Mark. "It hurts too much."

This was the horrible reality: Del Pretty was dying, one layer at a time. Few of us could witness such a thing.

But the love between son and father is like God's muscle. So while his teammates worked out back in Los Angeles, Mark Messner came to Harper Grace hospital every morning, 10 A.M., two hours before visiting time, to bathe his father.

He would lift him with his powerful arms and slide him gently into the tub. Sheets of bloody skin would stick to his hands, get under his fingernails. He did not flinch. He poured cool water over his father's body and comforted him. While Del could still speak, Mark held the phone to his ear and let him talk to the office at Hammell Music, the piano store which he owned in Livonia. Together they went over the books of the church, where Del was treasurer.

When Del's vocal cords no longer worked, Mark did the talking. When Del's eyesight went, Mark would tell him what he was missing.

On November 25, they put the Michigan–Ohio State game on TV. Del stayed awake for the entire thing. When the final gun sounded, Mark said "Hey, Dad! How about that? They're going to the Rose Bowl!"

Del raised his arm and made a soft fist. He shook it once.

Two days later, he died.

Mark knew as soon as the phone rang. It was 4 A.M. His mother was crying in the other room. "Mom," he whispered, "they said Dad expired."[5]

He paused.

"It makes him sound like a license plate."

At the funeral, Mark read a poem Del had sent him this fall. And when they closed the casket, Mark's Rose

---

[5]to breathe one's last breath

Bowl watch was around his father's wrist. Before it was always Del taking care of business matters, but now Mark handled the arrangements. He signed the papers. He went through the bills. He re-read the old letters and thought about their final moments together in the hospital, the feeding, the bathing. The circle was complete. The child had become father to the man.

"You know," Messner says now. "I was never embarrassed in the hospital. All that blood and skin, that was just his body. It was his heart that I was dealing with. I would have done anything for him. Anything."

*   *   *

Today, Mark will play a football game for the Rams, the regular season finale.

When it is over he will go to call his father, as he always did. And instead, he will have to close his eyes and imagine. "I know he's watching," he says without sadness. "He used to joke about having a beer with God. I'll bet he's doing it now."

You hear about the decline of the American family, how the old are tossed aside by the young. And then you hear of a kid who left pro football to tend to his dying father. These are the last words of the poem Del wrote, which Mark read at his funeral:

"If all else in a man's life added to zero, no greater success than to be counted his son's hero."

Isn't life funny? It takes us and leaves us. And love endures. Monday is Christmas, and that means this: Count your blessings, everybody, count them all very carefully. One precious person at a time.

How do you celebrate a new baby in your family? Many families have showers, buy gifts, and share the joy of new life when a baby is born.

Billie Jean Young had her first baby at fifteen. Unmarried, she was rejected by her church and her community as an "unwed mother."

Today, she is an assistant professor at Jackson State University in Mississippi. She could not have achieved this success without the help of a loving mother.

In this reading, Billie Jean Young shows her appreciation for her mama who helped her raise her two sons. Together they pass on a legacy of love as each new baby is born into the family.

Mama's Legacy

From *Essence* Magazine
Billie Jean Young

As I tore open the large envelope with the military address the week before Christmas, a precious gift fell out. It was a picture of my son, his wife and their new baby. My eldest child, Anthony, child of my childhood, now had a child. Tears came to my eyes as I thought about my son and the era of his birth.

I was 15 years old when Anthony was born. Cotton was still king in Alabama, and the summer after his birth I picked my first 200 pounds; the four-dollar compensation bought a case of milk for my baby.

Although the cotton rows seemed to stretch forever in the merciless heat of that late August sun, I persevered.[1] I had to prove myself to Mama. If I showed her how serious I was, she had promised to let me finish high school in the fall.

In 1963 there was such a stigma attached to having a child outside marriage that the emotional hurdles nearly overshadowed the practical ones. First there was the church. After my son was born, a deacon came to our house to let me know I had been "turned out" of the congregation. Then there was the community. In my conservative African-American sharecropping community, you had "broken your leg" and had a disability. At school you were spoiled—"tainted" is the word that always comes to mind, and it describes how I felt. Back then there were no gentle phrases like "teen parent" or "single parenting." You were an unwed mother. Period. And it could affect you economically. In high school I was a skilled typist with excellent grammatical skills. In those days, being a secretary was a plum job, and employers could skim for the very best. Upon graduating at 16, I had been promised a job as a secretary, but I was told that I was "too young" a few days before I was to start work. I didn't buy it, especially as my prospective employer had been so impressed with my skills. I had managed to graduate from high school and was capable and old enough to work. I knew what the real reason was: It was my child. I was devastated.[2]

I immersed myself in a strict religion that imposed celibacy[3] and frowned on education. I emerged after nearly four years and began to live again, but I was still

---

[1]continued in spite of obstacles
[2]made helpless; overwhelmed
[3]refrain from sexual intercourse

unschooled in sexual matters. I had my second son, Keith, when I was 19. Financial support from my boys' fathers was never forthcoming, so I realized early that I would have to go it alone. It was a sobering notion. I talked to Mama, and she was supportive. She agreed to keep the boys while I went off to work. My children became as much hers as mine. They call me Billie; they call my mother Mama.

Although her financial resources were limited, Mama allowed me to be a part-time parent. I took a full-time job, went to college and graduated from law school. I was responsible for feeding and clothing my kids, and when I was at home I took care of their physical needs. My siblings[4] sometimes said that I was "burdening" my mother with my children. I knew they wanted me to quit school, claim my children and get a job teaching or doing something else. But Mama never said anything. She was always proud of me and of whatever I did.

Mama paved the way for me to become a productive, whole person. I always knew that she was in the background cheering me on, so I pursued my goals with confidence. I felt a special urgency to succeed at whatever I was doing because so much was at stake and I knew I had no time to waste. I had been given a second chance, and I was determined to take it.

My mother wasn't as fortunate. Widowed at 37, she took her seven children and moved to be near her own parents, and they helped her raise us as she later helped me raise my sons. My boys are the recipients[5] of my mother's legacy—her love and devotion to us. They will pass that legacy down to their children as I have passed it down to them.

---

[4]brothers and sisters
[5]ones who receive

Christmas is a special time for my family. Everybody shares trials, tribulations, triumphs, hopes, and aspirations. Showing the pictures of my son and his baby to everyone will be a special treat for me this year. I am "Mama" now, and I'm eager to lavish my grandchild with his great-grandmother's legacy. Those photographs give life and image to the fact that I, Billie Jean, have raised a boy-child who has made a family. It is my mother's triumph as well as my own.

Nolan Ryan was born in 1947, and it seems as if he has played baseball ever since. From his early days in Little League, he has risen to being one of the best major league pitchers in history. From the 1960s to the 1990s, he played with the Mets, the Angels, the Astros, and the Texas Rangers.

Nolan Ryan is one of the greatest pitchers of all time and is known for his fastball. He leads all other pitchers in strikeouts. As of 1991, he had seven career no-hitters, more than any pitcher in history.

In this part of his autobiography, Nolan Ryan describes some happy childhood memories of his home in Alvin, Texas.

Alvin, Texas

From *Throwing Heat*
Nolan Ryan

My brother, Robert, was something of a hero to me, being a few years older and more advanced in athletics. I'd hang around with Robert and his friends, shag flies for them, sometimes get into a game when they were shy a player. I'd practice a lot with Robert in our backyard. We would pitch to each other. He'd catch me, and I'd catch him.

My first organized sports experience was in Little League. The first field in Alvin was cleared and built by my dad and the other fathers of the kids in the program. I played Little League from the time I was nine years old until I was thirteen. Some of my fondest memories of baseball come from those years.

I had heard that my dad was a pretty fair ball-player in his time during the Depression. Although he never was involved in any organized sports, he had a lot of natural athletic ability. As a Little League parent, he was always there when I needed him, but he was not like some of the others you hear about, the kind who meddle in games and care more about their kids winning than how they play the game. My dad was just interested in my having a good organized sports experience. Whenever I played ball, Dad would always stay in the background and just take everything in.

Making the Little League team was a thrill for all of us kids in Alvin. When we'd get our caps and uniforms, we'd be so proud, we'd wear the caps to school. That was a big deal. We played our games in the Texas heat in those old heavy flannel uniforms, but no one seemed to pay the weather any heed.

I was a good player, not a great player, although I did pitch a no-hitter in Little League and was on the All-Star team as an eleven- and twelve-year-old. I didn't develop great pitching velocity[1] until my sophomore year in high school. What I could always do, though, was throw a ball farther than the other kids—not harder, just farther. When I was a high school sophomore, I won a contest in a physical education class by throwing a heavy softball 309 feet. But my arm twinged a bit, and I realized I could get hurt doing that. I never threw a ball for distance again.

As Little Leaguers, we always fantasized about playing in the Little League World Series in Williamsport, Pennsylvania. That made making the All-Stars even more exciting. And although our team never went far in tournament play, we always had high expectations.

---

[1]speed

One year, after our team had been eliminated, I remember standing out on the field for the closing ceremony. The man who was presenting the awards gave a little talk to all of us. "One day," he said, "one of you Little Leaguers will go on to play in the major leagues."

When I heard what he said, it was like a bell went off in my head. I became very excited.

When I got home I told my mom about the ceremony and what the man said. "Mom," I said, "that man was talking about me."

"What do you mean?" she asked.

"It's me that he meant, Mom! I'm sure it was me he was talking about."

I remember that experience as vividly as if it just happened yesterday—the sun, the standing in the field, the man's voice, his words. I never forgot it. It was a monumental[2] thing in my mind.

During that period of my life, whenever I had the chance I would be throwing something, and my mother was always on me for breaking windows or hitting the car. I especially liked going down to Mustang Bayou near our house to throw rocks at the water moccasins and turtles.

Growing up in Alvin allowed me to have a childhood that was uncomplicated and without pressures. And although there were financial pressures on my dad, we always had the things we needed. We grew up not having a lot of extra things but not in want of any either. It was pretty much that way for most all the kids. But my father paid me for the newspaper route, and I mowed yards in the summer, so that I always had money for what I wanted.

---

[2] huge; very great

Since my dad worked so much, the burden fell on Mom to manage the household. For a time, with eight of us there sleeping two in a room, that was quite a chore. But she was always organized, and the house ran smoothly. Mom was a reserved person, but she was always open with all the kids, ready to talk over any of our problems.

It was a pleasant atmosphere to grow up in. We were all raised to respect other people, to do the right thing, to stand up for our rights, to value the family.

My parents' work ethic and dedication shaped my work ethic and dedication, both to my family and to my pitching. My goal has always been to raise my kids in the same kind of atmosphere that I grew up in—a family doing things for each other and loving each other.

REFLECT ·

How does Mark Messner become "father to the man" in his relationship with Del Pretty? Are the roles between parents and children sometimes reversed? Explain how this might happen.

How did Billie Jean Young's mother help give her a second chance? Do you know a mother and daughter with a similar relationship?

Which writer examines the traditional family structure? Which two writers show nontraditional family structures? Explain.

What personal goal does Nolan Ryan have as a father concerning his children?

WRITE ·

Mark Messner thought of Del Pretty as his father. Describe someone who is not related by blood but is like family to you.

Nolan Ryan vividly remembers the day the Little League announcer predicted Ryan's success in the major leagues. Write a journal entry about a childhood activity that affected your life's direction.

Is there anything unique about your family? Write a paragraph explaining what makes it special.

Stonecutter Carol Hazel working on stone for the Cathedral Church of St. John the Divine in Manhattan

PRIDE IN WORK

Are you happy in your work? Do you look forward to going to work or to the way you spend each day?

Most people must work to make money in order to provide health and happiness. Some people are simply "satisfied" with their jobs. Others love their jobs and are spending their days doing work they consider important to themselves as well as to others.

The following readings are about people who truly enjoy what they do for a living. They have pride in their work and think their lives have meaning—a purpose. Most important, they feel good about themselves and the effect they have on the future.

As you read, think about why each person works so hard and feels good about himself or herself.

Carol Hazel is a woman who loves her job. By learning new skills, she is able to do work that she finds important and enjoyable. She looks forward to going to work each day where she puts on a hard hat and cuts stone—stone that will last for generations.

This first-person account tells why Carol Hazel feels good about herself and the changes she has made in her life. It also tells why she feels such pride about the type of work she does.

I Feel Free

From *Cathedral*
Carol Hazel

I was born in New York City—13 when I got pregnant with my first, 16 with my second, 19 with my third, 21 when I had the fourth—a baby raising babies. But now the factory's closed; I got an operation. And I'm raising my children well, lifting myself up, doing it without public assistance, all because I'm here at the Cathedral Church of St. John the Divine in Manhattan cutting stone.

For a while I worked in a factory in the Bronx making jewelry boxes. The chemical fumes made you sick—no masks—and other people all angry that you're willing to work overtime because you have to. I also worked at a bar. There was a little stage next to the bar, with a go-go girl always dancing. It made me feel ashamed somehow.

But welfare was the worst. The constant documents: one for each kid. "What's this, what's that?" People going into your stomach for all this information. You are not your own person. Finally, two years ago I went to the welfare office for a "face-to-face," a recertification[1] procedure. I got real depressed. Then I saw the time had come. I just turned around.

I went to a school that taught mainly construction work. After 12 weeks of training and working on reading and writing, I found myself here at the Cathedral, working under the guidance of English craftsmen.

The stone got me. It fascinated me the first time I saw it. I saw the guys working there and thought, *I can do that*. And before I knew it I'm sitting in front of this stone.

It comes from the sea, from layers and layers of sedimentary[2] rock. It smells when you cut it, a fishy odor, from everything that's settled inside. It has the odor of ages coming to you from way back in time.

Now I'm married to my stone. I talk to it. I pray for the stone to come out right. I pray for straight lines. Sunday night I can't sleep, Monday morning I can't wait to get to work. At 8 A.M. I'm there with my tools, my chisel and my mallet, which are my prize possessions.

The work is very basic. It takes a good eye and a steady hand; you learn control. You see the stone, square it, get the center line which gives you a true face. Then you cut away waste: get in close, patience.

This is a good job for a woman. I don't have to sit behind a desk and worry about my boss's coffee

---

[1] updating documents and paperwork
[2] containing matter deposited by water or wind

or wife. I'm a stonecutter. I put on my jeans, boots, and hard hat. And the men respect me, I respect them. At lunch you'll find us playing dominoes together.

What it's really about is a need to be known. I'm Carol to myself. But now I'm Carol to others, not Carol going someplace to get money I didn't have the chance to earn. I feel free now, like having a hump off your back, or an ache you don't need.

And I find pride in my work. I know my boasting[3] pattern is going to be on that stone, way up in the sky. "That's my stone," I'll be able to say to my grandchildren. And I'll do this job right.

---

[3]shaping stonework with a broad chisel

Charles Kuralt is a television personality and author who presents stories about interesting people. He travels all over the country interviewing people. He traveled to the backwoods of Arkansas to interview Eddie Lovett.

This interview is the conversation between the two men. Lovett's "job"—his life's work—is reading. Kuralt asks Lovett to discuss what he reads and why.

Scholar of the Piney Woods

From *On the Road with Charles Kuralt*
Charles Kuralt

Eddie Lovett lives at the end of a long dirt road in the piney woods of Arkansas. There wasn't much to see when we got there: a couple of unpainted houses, the beginnings of a garden enclosed by a broken-down fence. But one thing we didn't expect: a shack with a tin roof, bearing an inscription: HIC HABITAT FELICITAS—Here lives happiness.

You'd expect the man who lives here to be a dirt farmer, or maybe a self-taught carpenter, a doer of odd jobs. And Eddie Lovett is all of those. Then how to explain that inscription in Latin over his door? Well, because Eddie Lovett—who never finished high school, and who lives with his children in near poverty out in the woods—is also a formidable[1] scholar. He has a library: a lifetime accumulation of thousands of books which he reads day and night. They have trans-

---

[1]awe-inspiring in excellence

formed the unlettered[2] son of a sharecropper into an educated man.

KURALT: What are you reading right now?

LOVETT: I'm reading space—about the great astronauts. I writes them pretty frequently; they writes me. And I admires their courage because I am a amateur, self-taught astronomer myself. I've sat on rooftops of barns many nights. That's what I'm studying right now. I am studying space.

     Didn't study last night 'cause I worked up to two thirty this morning, trying to get this place halfway presentable for you all to try to make pictures of it.

KURALT: How much time do you spend reading each day, now?

LOVETT: Out of twenty-four hours, I average twelve of them reading.

KURALT: Are you a fast reader?

LOVETT: Not too fast. I'm a slow, steady reader. I ponders[3] as I go along.

KURALT: What about literature? What about fiction?

LOVETT: Well, I don't like that too well, but one of my writers I like—I like James Baldwin. I likes him. He's good. I don't like all of his books, but I like some of them: *Go Tell It on the Mountain*, *The Fire Next Time*, things of that nature. I like some of that.

KURALT: Who are your favorite authors?

LOVETT: Oh, Lord! They're too numerous to name. But I will name a few. Oh, Lord!

---

[2]ignorant; uneducated
[3]think deeply; consider carefully

René Descartes, the great French philoso-
pher—"I think therefore I am."

And Socrates! Now, Socrates, you know, he
really didn't do any writing. He's known as the
father of logic, even if he didn't do any writing.

I am a lover of literature and a lover of knowledge.

Of course, Shakespeare, to my way of thinking, he's the greatest of them all—William Shakespeare. I got the complete works. I have it right
here in forty volumes. I think he was the greatest
that ever lived. That's in my judgment. Now, some
people think otherwise.

KURALT: But what good has all this reading done to
you? You're still living out here in the piney
woods.

LOVETT: Well, you know, a man is happy wherever he
loves and I love to read. I like to be quiet. And the
country is about the best place that I can find
quietness to read and study and research like I
desire. And I think that it's doing me—particularly
my children—a lot of good, because the truth to
tell, I'm really living for my children. I want to set
good examples for them. And the only way I can
get my children to do things that I would like for
them to do constructive, I have to set the example.

I don't think I've lost anything by gaining
knowledge, because I've been told by my father
and also by other people throughout the world
that man's greatest enemy is his ignorance. And so
by me pondering in my library, researching, I
have declared war upon my ignorance. And the
more I learn, the more I learn that I need to learn,
and the more I learn that I *don't* know. And I
aspires to drink very deep from the fountain of
knowledge.

Eddie Lovett steps to the door of his library each afternoon to watch his children come home from school. He gave the children names he discovered in his reading: Joanna, one of the women who discovered Jesus' empty tomb; Enima, a name suggested by Nietzsche; Yuri, for Yuri Gagarin, the Russian cosmonaut. He says his children are his greatest happiness. It pleases him that they all like to read nearly as much as he does, and that while he hasn't been able to give them much, the knowledge that they'll always have the library is a deep satisfaction to him.

LOVETT: Children maturing—great! They'll be men and women someday.

      Hic Habitat Felicitas—here lives happiness.

Following the publication of this interview, Eddie Lovett's library burned, destroying every book he owned. When the news media publicized the story of the fire, Eddie received letters and books from all over the world—8,000 books from 30 states and 5 countries. He received books from Lady Bird Johnson, widow of President Johnson; from children and college students; and from people who traveled to see him.

Lucy Lim was interviewed for a book about women who work in nontraditional jobs—jobs that have, in the past, been done by men only. Lucy Lim discusses her family background, her previous jobs, and the barriers she has had to overcome in order to achieve success. She enjoys her work and is proud of the progress she has made for herself and for other women.

Lucy Lim: Utility Switch Operator

Shelley D. Coleman
From *Hard-Hatted Women*
Edited by Molly Martin

I've worked in the trades since 1977. My first nontraditional job was in an open-pit copper mine in Arizona. I started there in an entry-level position as a laborer on a labor gang of ten or twelve people. Two of the others were women. The company was pushing affirmative action, because it had a class-action suit brought against it by a group of women in the mines in 1973. I was hired four years after the suit was filed, but even then, there were only a few women working for the company.

Being one of the first women was hard, and I didn't always have a comeback for every put down. But I held my own. I remember an incident involving a real macho guy on the labor gang who was hired around the same time I was. We were in the lunch room, and a discussion started up about whether women belonged in the mines or not. This guy believed women had no business in the mines, that it was a man's job. I said to him, "Hey, Sanders, what's your problem? I'm five-foot-two and 120 pounds. We're doing the same job shoveling and sweeping dirt and rock. Our shovels are the same size, and you can only put so much dirt in it. Just because you're bigger doesn't mean you can put more dirt on your shovel. They don't make bigger shovels for bigger guys." As I looked at his mouth hanging open, I thought, "Hey, yeah, this feels good. You macho guys may be bigger, but your brain is so much smaller that I can outthink you." A person my size has them so threatened. I used to tell them, "You guys go home to your wives and tell them about all the hard work you've done to maintain that macho myth about miners having to be six-foot-four and 250 pounds." It is pretty physical work, but you're not limited by your size. I worked there for five years, until the mine shut down. I'd still be there if it hadn't.

I grew up in an interracial marriage; my father is Chinese and my mother is Mexican. I have an older brother and a younger sister. I had a happy childhood, and I have fond memories of growing up in Arizona. My mom and dad ran a small corner grocery store, and we lived in the back. I went to school, came home, and there they were, every day. The store was open nine to nine. My dad was very Chinese in that he was a strict disciplinarian and really emphasized the importance of education. He had come here as an immigrant at age fifteen. He tried to go to school in Arizona but he was placed in a class with six- and seven-year-olds and felt so uncomfortable that he couldn't continue. My mother only went to ninth grade, so she agreed with my father about the emphasis on education. I knew at a young age that my brother, sister, and I were going to college in order to get good jobs.

I was pretty assertive as a child. My brother and I used to box together. I used to do a lot of rough playing—the kind that usually just boys were allowed to do. My brother never had a problem with me being a girl. He used to be a leader in the neighborhood; he was always team captain and would pick me to be on his teams—football, baseball, basketball. He has the same respect for me now as an adult.

After college, I worked as a retail clerk. Then I decided to get a job in the mines. My dad couldn't understand why I left a well-paying job at six dollars an hour as a retail clerk to go work in the copper mine for a quarter more an hour. I felt there were more promotion possibilities in the mines, and I also wanted to work outside and be more physical. I was twenty-seven and married at the time. The guys at the mine would complain, "Why don't you stay at home and take care of your husband? Your husband works, so you're taking someone else's job." I'd tell them, "I have a right to a job, regardless of my marital status. Also, I can't depend on my husband being there all the time. What if I wasn't married at all?" My co-workers and I had a number of verbal battles.

Now I work in San Francisco for Pacific Gas and Electric (PG&E), a private utility company. For the past four and a half years, I've been a systems operator, or switch operator. We work in the electrical substations, where we do high voltage electrical switching and operate circuit breaker disconnects. Not all substations are automatic, so when PG&E electrical maintenance crews need to work on equipment, our job is to clear breakers or sections of line. To do this, we have to write a procedure tag to physically clear switching, so the crew can work on the de-energized line. We sometimes have to de-energize a whole neighborhood or even large areas of the city.

My union affiliation is International Brotherhood of Electrical Workers (IBEW) Local 1245. My starting wage as a trainee was ten dollars an hour. Hourly wages for journey-level craft workers vary according to the shift, but they are basically in the range of twenty dollars, plus we get a twenty-five percent discount on our utility bill and good benefits.

There are a few other women working in other stations in the city. The first woman switch operator in San Francisco has been promoted to a prestigious[1] job in PG&E. After working for the company for ten years, she's now assistant dispatcher and works in the company's brain center. Some of the guys said the reason she was up there was because she could type super-fast. There have been several men who've gone up to the top and then down in a few months. The pressure is tremendous. It makes me laugh to think of them rationalizing[2] away her intelligence.

I really enjoy my job. You never know what you're in for when you arrive at work. Once on the graveyard shift, when I was a few months into the job, I got an alarm from another substation in the field. All I knew from the alarm was that there was something wrong. It could have been anything from a false alarm to fire. I got into my truck, and off I went. On my way to the substation I heard on the truck radio that there had been an explosion in a manhole and an operator was on the way. That operator was me! When I got there, I ran into the control room and saw that the enunciator alarm lights were flashing all over the place. I turned off the alarm and checked the panel lights. Then I had to figure out what had happened. The explosion should have opened up a circuit breaker in the substa-

---

[1]important; high-level
[2]giving reasons for

tion, clearing the fault. Instead, the 34,000-volt breaker failed and caused other breakers to open. It took my entire shift, till six in the morning, to bring it back to normal. Luckily it happened at a time when no one was out in the field.

I have a lot of responsibility in this job. You really need to be careful not to turn a switch the wrong way or you can energize a line when someone is working on it. A worker once closed a ground switch on an energized line instead of opening it, which caused an explosion. Opening up circuit breakers can cause a huge power outage and damage to equipment. We're talking about 230,000 volts. The breakers themselves weigh hundreds of pounds. Some are huge—six to eight feet square, others are the size of a kitchen stove.

From doing nontraditional work, I've definitely become more confident—partly because I've topped out; I'm now journey level. I feel like I've really achieved something. What I'd like to do now is to gain more knowledge about my job. I feel fortunate to be working with a great group of guys now. Maybe it's just the times. It's the way it should be, that women are now less a novelty. But it hasn't always been easy dealing with the men.

I do have a support group, Blue Collar Asian Women, which feels real good. It's fun to share our stories and see how similar they are, to talk about how to survive on our jobs, trade comebacks to sexist and racist comments. It helps us feel like we belong. Wherever I go, I endure racism. Just one look at me and you surely see I'm not WASP.[3] I hear a lot of racist ethnic jokes and I never let the jokes slide. For example, when I worked in Shreveport, Louisiana, in an oil refinery, there were about twenty-five women out of three hun-

---

[3]White Anglo-Saxon Protestant

dred workers. I worked with a wonderful black woman named Viola. She was telling a joke which involved a Chinese male cook. I let Viola tell her joke, all along thinking, "What am I going to do?" And the thing was, it did have a funny punchline. So afterwards I told her, "That was a pretty funny joke, but it would be better if you didn't use the word 'Chinaman.' That's derogatory,[4] like using the word 'nigger.' Could you use 'Chinese cook,' or whatever; you could even forget about the idea of using a *Chinese* cook. Why not just say 'cook'?" Viola apologized and said she had never thought about that before.

My dad taught me to be independent, because he wasn't going to be around to take care of me forever. And he gave me strong cultural messages: "Have a lot of pride that you are Chinese, that you are Mexican, that you are both." He encouraged my self-esteem and confidence. He always stressed being happy in your work and being very good at it, no matter what you chose to do. My parents had a hard time with racism. They weren't allowed to get married in the state of Arizona in the 1940s, because there were laws banning interracial marriages. It wasn't because my mother was Mexican—because Mexicans were considered white—but because my father was Chinese. So they got married in Mexico. The schools I went to reinforced cultural stereotypes: Chinese kids were supposed to be submissive and well-behaved, smart, cute. I've seen the stereotypes work in other ways: for example, if a black woman and an Asian woman apply for the same physical labor job, the black woman often gets hired over the Asian woman because the Asian woman is supposed to be passive and weak, and the black

---

[4]belittling

woman aggressive and tough. These stereotypes are damaging to everyone.

Sometimes I wonder how I have survived working with men. On a one-to-one basis, it's okay, but when they're in a pack, watch out. Some of them tell me that I was hired because of affirmative action, that I am a token. I just say I don't care, it has to start somewhere, and there are going to be lots of other women after me! For all of us who are breaking ground for women to follow, we feel we have something to prove; it's a lot of pressure to bear. Sometimes I think we underestimate ourselves, but unfortunately we become Everywoman. We're no longer individuals; we represent the entire sex.

My attitude is important to my survival on the job. I'm happy about eighty percent of the time. I have no regrets. The ideal I strive for is not to subdue[5] my aspirations,[6] but to incorporate emotional freedom and creativity and be more of myself at work.

---

[5]hold down
[6]hopes, dreams

REFLECT ·

How does each person feel about his or her work? Give details from each reading.

How are the two women's jobs similar?

Carol Hazel says, "And I'm raising my children well, lifting myself up. . . ." Explain how each of the three people has lifted himself or herself up.

Do you know anyone who shares Eddie Lovett's love of reading and learning? Explain.

How has Lucy Lim's family background influenced her sense of self?

How are other people benefiting from the work done by each of the three people?

Two of the readings are told from a personal point of view. The other reading is an interview. Which form of writing do you think works better? Why?

WRITE ·

Are you happy in your work? Why or why not? Write a journal entry explaining how you feel about a typical work day.

Do you know someone who, like Carol Hazel, has lifted herself—or himself—up? How did the person overcome obstacles or make changes in his or her life? Write a letter to the person explaining how you feel about the accomplishments.

All three people learned new skills as they worked to improve their lives. As a result, each person gained personal freedom. Do you agree that education is the key to freedom? Write a few paragraphs describing how education has affected your life.

Who is the hardest-working person you know? In a paragraph, describe the person and why she or he is motivated to work so hard.

A homeless man lying on a snowy sidewalk near the
Washington Monument in the nation's capital

No Place Like Home

What does *home* mean to you? Is it where you live now? Do you still live in the area where you grew up, or have you moved several times during your life? There is an expression, "Home is where the heart is." It means that home is more of a feeling, not just a building that provides shelter. These readings are about people who have feelings about their homes—having them and losing them.

As you read, think about what you would do if you no longer had your home or apartment, or any place to live. Think about what you would do if you lost your job, or if your home was destroyed by fire or taken away from you because of urban renewal.

When white settlers moved westward and took over land for the United States government, the Indians were "relocated"—forced to move from their reservations—and given a new "home." The white men had no understanding of the Indian's culture, including their strong belief in the spiritual world or in the powers of nature. The Indians' land had been their home "forever." They believed that the white man was unjustly seizing their homeland. Celsa Apapas, a Cupeño Indian woman, spoke not only her own tribal language but also Spanish and English. She spoke to the white government council on behalf of the Indian people.

We Do Not Want Any Other Home

Celsa Apapas
From *Aboriginal American Oratory*
by Louis Thomas Jones, Ph.D.

We thank you for coming here to talk to us in a way we can understand. It is the first time anyone has done so. You asked us to think what place we like next best to this place, where we always lived. You see that graveyard out there? There are our fathers and our grandfathers. You see that Eagle-nest Mountain and that Rabbit-hole Mountain? When God made them, He gave us this place. We have always been here. We do not care for any other place. . . . If you give us the best place in the world, it is not so good for us as this. . . . This is our home. . . . We cannot live anywhere else. We were born here and our fathers are buried here. . . . We want this place and not any other. . . .

There is no other place for us. We do not want you to buy any other place. If you will not buy this place, we will go into the mountains like quail, and die there, the old people and the women and children. Let the Government be glad and proud. It can kill us. We do not fight. We do what it says. If we cannot live here, we want to go into the mountains and die. We do not want any other home.

Celsa Apapas's plea was not listened to. The Cupeño Indians were moved from their rich and beautiful lands in the San Luis Rey Valley region of California to the Pala Reservation, at the base of Mount Palomar.

Have you ever heard the expression, "It really hits home"? This means that something happened that really affected you or made you clearly understand.

Some columnists have written essays about homelessness, hunger, and poverty. They give their opinions and suggest changes that could be made in our society to cope with these problems.

Bob Greene's column deals with those issues, but it is a true story about "home." It's about something that happened when a home owner returned home from vacation, and it's about someone who does not have a home.

Stranger at the Table

From *Cheeseburgers: The Best of Bob Greene*
Bob Greene

It's hard to make any sense of this story; but then, it's becoming increasingly hard to make any sense of these times.

On a recent Saturday night a man named David Gambill was returning to his home in Richmond, Virginia. Gambill and his wife, Ayer, had been on a week's vacation to Massachusetts; now they were tired, and were anxious to get back to their own house.

They pulled into the driveway. Gambill opened the back door. It struck him right away that something was amiss.

There was food on the stove, and the food was cooking. Chow mein and six fish sticks. But there was no one in the kitchen.

Gambill told his wife to wait by the back door. He began to walk around his house. In a bathroom, he found that a window had been broken. Now he was sure that someone was in his house.

He went from room to room. Later his friends would tell him that he was crazy to do that; the friends would say that he should have gotten out of the house and called the police. But Gambill was determined to find out who was in his home.

He went into his son's bedroom. The door to his son's closet was closed. Gambill opened the door.

Sitting in the closet, huddled behind Gambill's son's rolled-up sleeping bag, was a bedraggled-looking[1] old fellow.

"He looked awful," Gambill said. "He needed a shave, and he was wearing what I can only describe as thrift-shop clothing. The thing I remember most clearly was his eyes. They were just staring back at me. I knew right away that I wasn't in any danger. In his eyes I saw fear—fear and relief that I wasn't going to hurt him."

Gambill stood there staring at the man. The man started to speak.

"I was hungry," the man said. "I was hungry, so I came on into your house."

Gambill didn't know what to say to the man.

"You can call the police if you want," the man said.

Gambill thought of what he should do: pounce on the man, tie him up, lock him in the closet.

But he realized that what he was feeling wasn't anger. It was sadness.

"You really broke in because you were hungry?" Gambill said.

---

[1]soiled, as if dragged through dirt

"Yes," the man said.

Gambill knew that, in looking around the house, nothing had been stolen. The only things that had been disturbed, with the exception of the broken bathroom window, were the chow mein and the fish sticks that had been taken from the Gambills' refrigerator and put on the stove.

"You can go in and finish your supper," Gambill said.

So the man straightened up, walked out of the closet, and went to the kitchen. As Gambill and his wife watched, the man put the chow mein and the fish sticks onto a plate, and sat down at the kitchen table.

Gambill, almost as a second thought, picked up the telephone and called the Henrico County police. He told the dispatcher what had happened; the dispatcher said police officers would be over immediately.

"I couldn't believe how fast he ate that food," Gambill said. "He just kept putting it into his mouth as fast as he could.

"I know I probably shouldn't have let him do it. But when I thought about it—he was risking getting arrested so he could have a meal. He was risking his life, really. He could have got shot breaking into someone's house. If he was that desperate, I couldn't deny him the food."

The man finished his meal. He went over and got a water tumbler from the Gambills' shelf. He drew a glass of water from the kitchen sink. He gulped it down.

Gambill said he still felt no danger, being in the house with the man who had broken in. "He wasn't going to spring at me or anything," Gambill said.

"There was no threat to me. He was very docile."[2]

The police arrived. They entered the Gambills' kitchen, and Gambill immediately filled them in on what had happened. The police stared at the man, who was still in the kitchen, with the now-empty plate and glass. The man made no effort to flee.

The police began to read the man his Miranda rights.

"It was the most bizarre scene," Gambill said. "The old guy was standing there, and the police were reading his rights to him, and it was like something off a television show. I kept staring at the old guy, and I kept hearing these phrases the police were reading: 'right to remain silent,' and 'right to an attorney.' The guy was showing no visible reaction."

The police put the man in handcuffs and led him out to the squad car. As the man left, he said nothing to Gambill or his wife. Later, the police would charge the man—whom they identifed as Allen Young, age approximately fifty-seven—with breaking and entering, and petty larceny.[3]

"I've felt terrible ever since that night," Gambill said. "I make a pretty good living; hunger isn't a big issue for me. We read about hunger, and we know it's out there, but it takes something like this to bring it home."

Gambill said that, in the days following the incident, he has gone through all the emotions that people who are burglarized often feel: a sense of violation, a sense of being helpless against outside forces, a sense

---

[2]easy to manage
[3]unlawful theft of personal property

of his home not being entirely his own any longer.

But the dominant emotion was a different one.

"I don't know how to put this, but I almost felt like crying," he said. "Crying at the thought of what's going on out there for people like that fellow. Can you understand what I'm saying? I haven't been sleeping very well at night."

On December 7, 1941, Japan attacked the United States base Pearl Harbor in Hawaii. The U.S. and Canada became suspicious of any person of Japanese heritage located on our west coast.

The author was a young child at the time. Her family was moved from Vancouver to an internment[1] camp 700 miles away in New Denver. As an adult, Shizuye Takashima became a leading artist in Canada. Her nonfiction book is illustrated by paintings that are pictures and words of her memories of prison camp. She writes in sentences that look more like poetry on the page.

Spring 1944

From *A Child in Prison Camp*
Shizuye Takashima

The war with Japan is getting very bad. I can feel my parents growing anxious. There is a lot of tension in the camp; rumors of being moved again, of everyone having to return to Japan. Kazuo and his family leave for Japan. Many are angry they have left us. Some call them cowards, others call them brave! I only feel sad, for I liked Kazuo so much, so very much.

Father shouts at mother, "We return to Japan!"
"But what are we going to do? You have your brothers and sisters there. I have no one. Besides, the children. . . ."

---

[1]detainment of people during war

"Never mind the children," father answers.
"They'll adjust. I'm tired of being treated as a spy,
a prisoner. Do what you like; I'm returning!"

I can see Mrs. Kono looks confused.
"My husband is talking of returning to Japan, too.
I think it's the best thing. All our relatives
are still there. We have nothing here."
Yuki stares at her. "It's all right for you, Mrs. Kono,
you were born there, but we weren't.
I'm not going. That's all!"
And she walks out of the house.

Mother gets very upset. I know she wants to cry.
"I don't want to go to Japan, either," I say.
"They're short of food and clothing there.
They haven't enough for their own people.
They won't want us back."

All of a sudden I hate that country for having started
the war. I say aloud, "Damn Japs! Why don't they
stop fighting?" Father glares. "What do you mean
'Japs'? You think you're not a Jap? If I hear you say that
again I'll throttle[2] you." I see anger and hatred in his
eyes.

I leave the room, go out of the house. I hear him
say loudly to mother, "It's all your fault. You poison our
children's minds by saying we're better off here."

And another argument starts. I am getting tired
of it, and confused. I feel so helpless, and wish
again I were older, then maybe I could go somewhere.

---

[2]to choke or strangle

. . . But I do not hate the people in Japan. I know
Yuki doesn't hate them either, really.
It's all so senseless. Really, maybe children should
rule the world! Yuki tells me it is wrong for father,
because of his anger at the wrong done towards him
and us, to expect us to return to his country:
"Sure, we're Japanese. But we think like Canadians.
We won't be accepted in Japan if we go there."

*At the end of the war, the Takashima family relocated to
Toronto.*

"Homelessness" does not have to be a problem. It is the result of many problems—ones we have yet to solve. Millions of people are homeless—in the richest country in the world.

Some people are homeless because they have no resources. When people do not have the education or skills or good health to get jobs, they have no money. When people have no money, they cannot find a place to live or food to eat or clothes to cover them. . . .

Some people are homeless due to natural disasters such as flood and fire. Some are homeless because a family illness or tragedy has taken all of their resources— their money and their emotional stability. Some women and children are homeless because they cannot go home to violent husbands or fathers. Some are homeless because they are mentally ill and have no place to go. And some—a growing number—are children.

This reading is the powerful introduction to a book about homelessness.

Ordinary People

From *Rachel and Her Children*
Jonathan Kozol

He was a carpenter. She was a woman many people nowadays would call old-fashioned. She kept house and cared for their five children while he did construction work in New York City housing projects. Their home was an apartment in a row of neat brick buildings. She was very pretty then, and even now, worn down by months of suffering, she has a lovely, wistful look. She wears blue jeans, a yellow jersey, and a bright red ribbon in her hair—"for luck," she says. But luck has not been with this family for some time.

They were a happy and chaotic[1] family then. He was proud of his acquired skills. "I did carpentry. I painted. I could do wallpapering. I earned a living. We spent Sundays walking with our children at the beach." They lived near Coney Island. That is where this story will begin.

"We were at the boardwalk. We were up some. We had been at Nathan's. We were eating hot dogs."

He's cheerful when he recollects that afternoon. The children have long, unruly hair. They range in age from two to ten. They crawl all over him—exuberant[2] and wild.

Peter says that they were wearing summer clothes: "Shorts and sneakers. Everybody was in shorts."

When they were told about the fire, they grabbed the children and ran home. Everything they owned had been destroyed.

---

[1] in a confused or disordered condition
[2] full of life

"My grandmother's china," she says. "Everything." She adds: "I had that book of gourmet cooking . . ."

What did the children lose?

"My doggy," says one child. Her kitten, born three days before, had also died.

Peter has not had a real job since. "Not since the fire. I had tools. I can't replace those tools. It took me years of work." He explains he had accumulated tools for different jobs, one tool at a time. Each job would enable him to add another tool to his collection. "Everything I had was in that fire."

They had never turned to welfare in the twelve years since they'd met and married. A social worker helped to place them in a homeless shelter called the Martinique Hotel. When we meet, Peter is thirty. Megan is twenty-eight. They have been in this hotel two years.

She explains why they cannot get out: "Welfare tells you how much you can spend for an apartment. The limit for our family is $366. You're from Boston. Try to find a place for seven people for $366 in New York City. You can't do it. I've been looking for two years."

The city pays $3,000 monthly for the two connected rooms in which they live. She shows me the bathroom. Crumbling walls. Broken tiles. The toilet doesn't work. There is a pan to catch something that's dripping from the plaster. The smell is overpowering.

"I don't see any way out," he says. "I want to go home. Where can I go?"

A year later I'm in New York. In front of a Park Avenue hotel I'm facing two panhandlers.[3] It takes a moment before I can recall their names.

---

[3]beggars on the street

They look quite different now. The panic I saw in them a year ago is gone. All five children have been taken from them. Having nothing left to lose has drained them of their desperation.

The children have been scattered—placed in various foster homes. "White children," Peter says, "are in demand by the adoption agencies."

Standing here before a beautiful hotel as evening settles in over New York, I'm reminded of the time before the fire when they had their children and she had her cookbooks and their children had a dog and cat. I remember the words that Peter used: "We were up some. We had been at Nathan's." Although I am not a New Yorker, I know by now what Nathan's is: a glorified hot-dog stand. The other phrase has never left my mind.

Peter laughs. "Up some?"

The laughter stops. Beneath his street-wise manner he is not a hardened man at all. "It means," he says, "that we were happy."

REFLECT ··································

Did David Gambill do the right thing by calling the police when he found the man in his home? What would you have done in his situation?

What reasons does Celsa Apapas, the Cupeño Indian woman, give for not wanting to leave her home?

In "Spring 1944," Shizuye Takashima says, "Really, maybe children should rule the world!" What causes her to make this statement?

Which of the readings do you find the saddest? Why?

Why do you think Jonathan Kozol called his introduction "Ordinary People"? How are Peter, Megan, and their children ordinary?

Was Shizuye Takashima Japanese or Canadian? Explain your answer.

What is Bob Greene's purpose in writing "Stranger at the Table"? Which do you think is more effective—a story showing an example, or an essay giving facts and opinions?

WRITE ·

Do you know people who have lost their homes? Explain what happened and how they coped.

Jonathan Kozol writes about people who were "up some" but who are now "down and out." Do you know anyone who, for some reason, was down and out but who survived and is living better now?

Have you ever been approached by someone begging for money to buy food? Write a journal entry with details of what happened when you were approached and how you reacted and felt.

Shizuye Takashima's father states to her mother, "Never mind the children. . . . They'll adjust." Do you agree that children adjust easily to a new home or to other changes? Give examples.

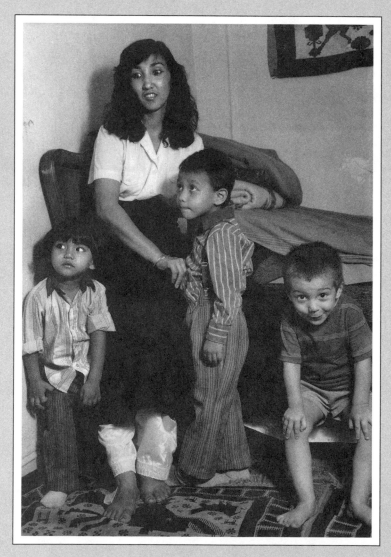

An Afghan mother and her children sharing a light moment

TIME OUT TO LAUGH

Do you sometimes take life too seriously, or do you have a good sense of humor even when things are not going well?

You might hear someone say, "Lighten up!"—a term that suggests that you try to take life less seriously. Life is more enjoyable if you can see the humor in everyday situations.

All three readings are by authors who share a lighter view of the world. They write with a sense of humor, and they describe times when they needed to laugh at life a little.

As you read, think about your need to take time out to laugh once in a while.

Shirley Jackson is the author of the classic short story "The Lottery."

This reading is from a book about her children, referred to lovingly as "savages." Jackson recalls an exciting moment for her family. With a sense of humor, she explains her children's various reactions to something they do not quite understand.

A New Arrival

From *Life Among the Savages*
Shirley Jackson

It was a beautiful morning, cold and clear and full of color, and the taxi driver was just finishing a story about how his wife's mother had come to visit them and canned all the peaches his wife had been planning to put into their freezer. "Just wasted the whole lot of them," he said, and pulled up in front of the house with a flourish.

"There are the children on the porch," I said.

"Beginning to seem like Christmas," my husband said to the taxi driver as I got out, and the taxi driver said, "Snow before morning."

Jannie's hair had obviously not been combed since I left, and as I went up the front walk I was resolving to make her tell immediately where she had hidden the hairbrush. She was wearing her dearest summer sundress, and she was barefoot. Laurie needed a haircut, and he had on his old sneakers, one of which no longer laces, but fastens with a safety pin;

I had made a particular point of throwing those sneakers into the garbage can before I left. Sally had chocolate all over her face and *she* was wearing Laurie's fur hat. All three of them were leaning over the porch rail, still and expectant.[1]

I tried to catch hold of all three of them at once, but they evaded[2] me skillfully and ran at their father. "Did you bring it?" Jannie demanded, "did you bring it, did you bring it, did you bring it?"

"Is *that* it you're carrying?" Laurie demanded sternly, "that *little* thing?"

"Did you *bring* it?" Jannie insisted.

"Come indoors and I'll show you," their father said.

They followed him into the living room, and stood in a solemn row by the couch. "Now don't touch," their father said, and they nodded all together. They watched while he carefully set the bundle down on the couch and unwrapped it.

Then, into the stunned silence which followed, Sally finally said, "What is it?"

"It's a baby," said their father, with an edge of nervousness to his voice, "it's a baby boy and its name is Barry."

"What's a baby?" Sally asked me.

"It's pretty small," Laurie said doubtfully. "Is that the best you could get?"

"I tried to get another, a bigger one," I said with irritation, "but the doctor said this was the only one left."

"My goodness," said Jannie, "what are we going to do with *that*? Anyway," she said, "*you're* back."

---

[1]waiting
[2]avoided; got away from

Suddenly she and Sally were both climbing onto my lap at once, and Laurie came closer and allowed me to kiss him swiftly on the cheek; I discovered that I could reach around all three of them, something I had not been able to do for some time.

"Well," Laurie said, anxious to terminate[3] this sentimental[4] scene, "so now we've got this baby. Do you think it will grow?" he asked his father.

"It's got very small feet," Jannie said. "I really believe they're *too* small."

"Well, if you don't like it we can *always* take it back," said their father.

"Oh, we like it all right, I guess," Laurie said comfortingly. "It's only that I guess we figured on something a little bigger."

"What *is* it?" asked Sally, unconvinced. She put out a tentative[5] finger and touched one toe. "Is this its foot?"

"Please start calling it 'him' " I said.

"Him?" said Sally. "Him?"

"Hi, Barry," said Laurie, leaning down to look directly into one open blue eye, "hi, Barry, hi, Barry, hi, Barry."

"Hi, Barry," said Jannie.

"Hi, Barry," said Sally. "Is this your foot?"

"I suppose it'll cry a lot?" Laurie asked his father, man to man.

His father shrugged. "Not much else it *can* do," he pointed out.

"I remember Jannie cried all the time," Laurie went on.

---

[3] to end
[4] showing tender feelings; emotional
[5] timid; hesitant

"I did not," Jannie said. "*You* were the one cried all the time."

"Did you get it at the hospital?" Sally asked. She moved Barry's foot up and down and he curled his toes.

"Yes," I said.

"Why didn't you take me?" Sally asked.

"I took you the last time," I said.

"What did you say its name was?" Sally asked.

"Barry," I said.

"Barry?"

"Barry."

"Where did you get it?"

"Well," Laurie said. He sighed and stretched. "Better take a look at those Greek tetradrachms,"[6] he said.

"Right," said his father, rising.

"Jannie, you go find that hairbrush," I said.

Laurie, on his way out of the room, stopped next to me and hesitated, obviously trying to think of something congratulatory to say. "I guess it *will* be nice for you, though," he said at last. "Something to keep you busy now *we're* all grown up."

---

[6]ancient Greek silver coins

You might recognize Andy Rooney. He has appeared at the end of "Sixty Minutes" for many years. He often begins his commentary, "Have you ever wondered about . . . ?" He is one of those writers with a good sense of humor who can present the funny side of most situations.

As Andy Rooney might say, "Have you ever thought about how much work you could get done on a Saturday if you had some help from . . . let's say . . . from the White House staff?"

Saturdays with the White House Staff

From *And More by Andy Rooney*
Andy Rooney

Every Saturday morning I make a list of Things to Do Today. I don't *do* them, I just make a list. My schedule always falls apart and I realize that what I need is the kind of support the President gets. Here's how Saturday would go for me if I had the White House staff home with me:

7:15–7:30—I am awakened by one of the kitchen staff bringing me fresh orange juice, toast, jam, and coffee.

7:30–7:45—The valet[1] lays out my old khaki pants, a clean blue denim shirt, and my old work shoes. I dress.

---

[1] an employee who lays out a person's clothes and helps in daily routines

7:45–8:00—The newspaper is on my desk, together with a brief summary of it prepared overnight by three editors.

8:00–8:15—My mail has been sorted with only the interesting letters left for me to read. Checks for bills have been written and stamps put on envelopes. All I have to do is sign them. The Secretary of the Treasury will make sure my checks don't bounce.

8:15–8:30—Staff maintenance men have left all the right tools by the kitchen sink, together with the right size washers. I repair the leaky faucet.

8:30–8:45—While I repaired the faucet, other staff members got the ladder out of the garage and leaned it against the roof on the side of the house. While two of them hold it so I won't fall, I clean out the gutters. They put the ladder away when I finish.

8:45–9:00—Manny, my own barber, is waiting when I get down from the roof and he gives me a quick trim.

9:00–9:15—Followed by four Secret Service operatives,[2] I drive to the car wash, where they see to it that I go to the head of the line.

9:15–9:30—On returning from the car wash, I find the staff has made a fresh pot of coffee, which I enjoy with my wife, who thanks me for having done so many of the little jobs around the house that she'd asked me to do. Two insurance salesmen, a real estate woman, and a college classmate trying to raise money call during this time, but one of my secretaries tells them I'm too busy to speak with them.

Long before noon, with my White House staff, I've done everything on my list, and I can relax, read a book, take a nap, or watch a ballgame on television.

---

[2]workers

I'm dreaming, of course. This is more the way my Saturdays *really* go:

6:00–7:30—I am awakened by a neighbor's barking dog. After lying there for half an hour, I get up, go down to the kitchen in my bare feet, and discover we're out of orange juice and filters for the coffee-maker.

7:30–8:30—I go back upstairs to get dressed, but all my clean socks are in the cellar. They're still wet because they weren't taken out of the washing machine and put in the dryer. I wait for them to dry.

8:30–9:30—Now that I have my shoes on, I go out to the driveway to get the paper. Either the paperboy has thrown it into the bushes again or he never delivered it. I drive to the news store and get into an argument about why the Raiders beat the Eagles.

9:30–10:30—The mail has come and I sit down in the kitchen to read it. The coffee was left on too high and is undrinkable. The mail is all bills and ads. I don't know how much I have in the bank, and I don't have any stamps. I don't feel like doing anything. I just sit there, staring.

10:30–11:30—I finally get up and go down to the cellar but can't find the right wrench for the faucet in the kitchen sink, and I don't have any washers anyway. I try to do it with pliers and string but finally give up.

11:30–12:30—I don't feel like digging the ladder out from behind the screens so I drive to the car wash, but there are twenty-three cars in front of me. Later, at the barbershop, Manny can't take me today.

I go home, get out of the car, and find the left front tire is soft. I go into the house and sit down to stare again as my wife comes in and complains that I never do anything around the house.

An important part of daily life is dealing with your children, if you have any, and trying to be the best parent you can be. For many years, people have associated Bill Cosby with "fatherhood." With five children and a doctorate in education, Bill Cosby knows a lot about children.

As a stand-up comic, Bill Cosby has often joked about his family life. He knows that no matter how different families are, there are some things they all share.

With some humor, Bill Cosby gives some serious advice about raising children. In this excerpt from his book, he discusses the special relationship between fathers and daughters.

In from the Cold

From *Fatherhood*
Bill Cosby

Some authority on parenting once said, "Hold them very close and then let them go." This is the hardest truth for a father to learn: that his children are continuously growing up and moving away from him (until, of course, they move back in). Such growth is especially bittersweet with a daughter because you are always in love with her. When she is very small, she comes to you and says, "Daddy, I have to go to the bathroom," and you proudly lead her there as if the toilet were a wedding chapel. You drop to your knees, unbutton her overalls, and lovingly put her on the seat.

And then one day it happens: she stops you from

unbuttoning her and pushes you away because she wants privacy in the bathroom. It is your first rejection by this special sweetheart, but you have to remember that it means no lessening of her love. You must use this rejection to prepare yourself for others that will be coming, like the one I received on a certain day when I called my daughter at college. Someone in her dorm picked up the phone and I asked to speak to my daughter. The person left and returned about a minute later to say, "She says she's sleeping right now."

I was hurt to have my daughter put me on hold, but intellectually I knew that this was just another stage in her growth; and I remembered what Spencer Tracy had said in *Father of the Bride*: "Your son is your son till he takes him a wife, but your daughter is your daughter for all of your life." You are stuck with each other, and what a lovely adhesion[1] it is.

There is no commitment in the world like having children. Even though they often will drive you to consider commitment of another kind, the value of a family still cannot be measured. The great French writer André Malraux said it well: "Without a family, man, alone in the world, trembles with the cold."

Yes, it is even better to have Jeffrey, that wee airborne terror, than to have no child at all. Just make sure that you travel in separate planes.

This commitment, of course, cannot be a part-time thing. The mother may be doing ninety percent of the disciplining, but the father still must have a full-time acceptance of all the children. He never must say, "Get these kids out of here; I'm trying to watch TV." If he ever does start saying this, he is liable to see one of his kids on the six o'clock news.

---

[1]attachment

Both mother and father have to work to establish an *honesty*. The child doesn't have to tell them *everything*, but he *should* be talking to his parents the same way he talks to someone who is not in charge of his life. When your son has his first wet dream, you don't want him to have it interpreted in the boys' locker room. And if your daughter's period is late, you want her to feel as comfortable going to you as to a confidante[2] at the mall.

Sometimes I tell my son that the meaning of his name is "Trust nobody and smile." But that certainly doesn't apply to his parents: my wife and I have tried to stay tuned in to him and the girls from the very beginning. We have shown all five of them constant attention, faith, and love. Like all parents since Adam and Eve (who never quite seemed to understand sibling rivalry[3]), we have made mistakes; but we've learned from them, we've learned from the *kids*, and we've all grown together. The seven of us will always stumble and bumble from time to time, but we do have the kind of mutual trust that I wish the United Nations had. And, with breaks for a little hollering, we smile a lot.

---

[2]a close friend who is trusted with one's secrets
[3]fighting and competition among brothers and sisters

REFLECT ····································

How does each of Shirley Jackson's children react to the new baby?

Like many parents, Jackson and her husband are a little nervous about bringing a new baby home. Why?

How is Andy Rooney's Saturday morning made easier when he receives imaginary help from the White House staff?

What parts of Bill Cosby's piece are funny? What parts are serious?

How does Jackson humorously describe each of her children when she sees them standing on the porch?

Shirley Jackson does not explain what *it* is immediately. Why do you think she does this?

WRITE ··

Imagine that the White House staff will help you for one morning. Contrast a typical day with the kind of day you could have with their help.

Do you think parents today worry too much or worry too little about their children? Choose one view and give examples.

Bill Cosby talks about how quickly our children grow up and move away from us. Given the lack of time, what values do you think parents should pass on to their children before the children move away?

Imagine that you are a child meeting a new baby brother or sister for the first time. Write a journal entry telling how you feel. What would you say to your parents about the baby?

Do you agree with Bill Cosby's statement that "we all make mistakes with our kids, but we can learn from them [mistakes] and grow with them [kids]"? Explain your views in a paragraph.

Martin Luther King, Jr., delivering his famous "I Have a Dream" speech in Washington, D.C., on August 28, 1963

VOICES FROM THE PAST

Have you ever wished you had lived in another time and place in history? What changes might you have taken part in if you lived during an earlier time?

Our history is rich in lessons that we can learn from. "History" simply means "his story" (and "her story"), recalling what happened to people in the past.

Each day the world changes because of the events that take place. While we make progress and look forward to the future, we give up something valuable from our past.

As you read, think about the changing world that each writer or speaker faces. Think about what each person lost and gained.

Black Hawk, who lived from 1767 to 1838, was a Sauk Indian known for fighting against white settlers moving west through Illinois. In 1804, the Sauk and Fox Indians agreed to give the United States the lands east of the Mississippi River. Black Hawk protested the contract, saying that the chiefs had been given liquor before they signed the documents.

Historians think that Black Hawk gave this speech when he was turned over to an Indian agent after losing the Black Hawk War. Black Hawk was imprisoned until 1833, when he was placed on a reservation near Des Moines. He died there in 1838.

Farewell to Black Hawk

From *Indian Oratory*
Chief Black Hawk

You have taken me prisoner, with all my warriors. I am much grieved; for I expected, if I did not defeat you, to hold out much longer, and give you more trouble before I surrendered. I tried hard to bring you into ambush, but your last general understood Indian fighting. I determined to rush upon you, and fight you face to face. I fought hard, but your guns were well aimed. The bullets flew like birds in the air, and whizzed by our ears like the wind through the trees in winter.

My warriors fell around me; it began to look dismal. I saw my evil day at hand. The sun rose dim on us in the morning, and at night it sank in a dark cloud, and looked like a ball of fire. That was the last sun that shone on Black Hawk. His heart is dead, and no longer beats quick in his bosom. He is now a prisoner to the white men; they will do with him as they wish. But he can stand torture, and is not afraid of death. He is no coward. Black Hawk is an Indian!

He has done nothing for which an Indian ought to be ashamed. He has fought for his countrymen, against the white men who came, year after year, to cheat them and take away their lands. You know the cause of our making war. It is known to all white men. They ought to be ashamed of it. The white men despise the Indians and drive them back from their homes. But the Indians are not deceitful.[1] The white men speak bad of the Indian, and look at him spitefully.[2] But the Indian does not tell lies. Indians do not steal. An Indian who is as bad as a white man could not live in our nation. He would be put to death and eaten by the wolves.

The white men are bad schoolmasters. They carry false looks and deal in false actions. They smile in the face of the poor Indian, to cheat him; they shake him by the hand to gain his confidence, to make him drunk, and to deceive him. We told them to let us alone, and keep away from us; but they followed on, and beset our paths, and they coiled themselves among us, like the snake. They poisoned us by their touch. We were not safe; we lived in danger. We were becoming like them, hypocrites and liars; all talkers and no workers.

We looked up to the Great Spirit. We went to our Father. We were encouraged. His great council gave us fair words and big promises; but we obtained no satis-

---

[1] willing to lie or mislead
[2] full of hate

faction. Things were growing worse. There were no deer in the forest. The opossum and the beaver were fled. The springs were drying up, and our people were without food to keep them from starving. We called a great council and built a big fire. The spirit of our fathers arose and spoke to us to avenge our wrongs or die. We set up the war whoop and dug up the tomahawk; our knives were ready, and the heart of Black Hawk swelled high in his bosom when he led his warriors to battle. He is satisfied. He will go to the world of spirits contented. He has done his duty. His father will meet him there and commend him. Black Hawk is a true Indian. He feels for his wife, his children, his friends, but he does not care for himself. He cares for the nation and for the Indians. They will suffer. He laments[4] their fate.

The white men do not scalp the head, they do worse—they poison the heart. It is not pure with them. His countrymen will not be scalped, but will in a few years be like the white men, so you cannot trust them; and there must be in the white settlements as many officers as men, to take care of them and keep them in order.

Farewell, my nation! Black Hawk tried to save you, and avenge your wrongs. He drank the blood of some of the whites. He has been taken prisoner, and his plans are stopped. He can do no more! He is near his end. His sun is setting, and he will rise no more. Farewell to Black Hawk!

---

[4]feels sorrow; grieves for

This recollection is from a book which records memories of people living in the Appalachian South. Appalachia is an area that extends from West Virginia and southeast Ohio to northern Georgia.

People in the region have made their livings farming or working in the coal mines or mills. Some live in poverty, and some towns have few residents because the young people have moved to cities. A land of pioneers and mountain men has had to adapt to a modern world.

Everette Tharp, an elderly Appalachian woman, speaks of her memories of a different way of life.

Memories of Appalachia

Everette Tharp
From *Voices from the Mountains*
Guy and Candie Carawan

I was born on June the thirteenth, 1899, in eastern Kentucky. I was raised on a farm with domestic and wild animals. Sheep, hogs, and cattle roamed wild in the forest. We raised what we ate and slept in dilapidated[1] houses. We enjoyed nature in all of its aspects and knew no doctors or surgeons. Mountain dew[2] was our principal medicine.

I knew the whistle of the ground hog, the call of the crow, the songs of the birds, the cunning of the fox, and the squall of the bobcat. I knew the art and

---

[1]broken down; shabby
[2]moonshine; homemade whiskey

expertise[3] of teaching an oxen to put his neck to the yoke and to kneel down low when his load was too heavy. These are things that can't be taught in the classroom.

The mountains of eastern Kentucky were a vast domain, rich in the abundance of nature to sustain domestic and wild animals. The timberlands, valleys, mountains, and streams were a Garden of Eden where the lamb lay down with the lion. There were no barbed-wire fences to restrain men. The mountain man knew how, as the Indian did, to live off the land. At this time there were no phonographs, no radios, no television, no automobiles, no railroads, no public highways, no airplanes. Our highways were buffalo trails made by wild animals and later on used by the Indians and white adventurers. Freight boats traveled the Kentucky River to transport the necessaries of life to Hazard and Whitesburg.

I lived through the aftermath of the mountain feuds when father was committed against son and brother against brother. I lived by the code of the mountains. I lived in an age when people respected honor and truth, where a liar was scorned and ridiculed and a man who would not pay his debts was considered an outcast.

When the railroad pushed up the valley from Jackson to Hazard and on to McRoberts, it marked the beginning of the end of a way of life for a group of rugged men and women who had the nerve and the courage to traverse[4] the mountain barriers and establish rugged individualism[5]—known as the mountain man.

---

³expert opinion or knowledge ⁴to travel across

⁵to lead life in one's own way

One of the most important speeches in American history was made on August 28, 1963. Martin Luther King, Jr., led the March on Washington by 200,000 black and white Americans. Their action was meant to urge Congress to pass President Kennedy's civil rights bill. King, a Baptist minister, used Biblical quotes and spoke with great emotion about his hopes and dreams for the future.

The Civil Rights Act of 1964 made racial discrimination in public places unlawful. It also called for equal opportunity in employment and education. As a result of King's leading nonviolent civil rights demonstrations, he won the Nobel Peace Prize in 1964. He continued to work for social justice until he was killed in 1968.

I Have a Dream

Martin Luther King, Jr.

. . . I say to you today, my friends, so even though we face the difficulties of today and tomorrow, I still have a dream. It is a dream deeply rooted in the American dream.

I have a dream that one day this nation will rise up and live out the true meaning of its creed: "We hold these truths to be self-evident; that all men are created equal."

I have a dream that one day, on the red hills of Georgia, sons of former slaves and the sons of former slaveowners will be able to sit down together at the table of brotherhood.

I have a dream that one day even the state of Mississippi, a state sweltering with the heat of injustice, sweltering with the heat of oppression, will be transformed into an oasis[1] of freedom and justice.

I have a dream that my four little children will one day live in a nation where they will not be judged by the color of their skin but by the content of their character.

I have a dream today.

I have a dream that one day, down in Alabama, with its vicious racists, with its governor having his lips dripping with the words of interposition[2] and nullification,[3] one day right there in Alabama, little black boys and black girls will be able to join hands with little white boys and white girls and walk together as sisters and brothers.

I have a dream today.

I have a dream that one day "every valley shall be exalted, every hill and mountain shall be made low, the rough places will be made plains, and the crooked places will be made straight, and the glory of the Lord shall be revealed, and all flesh shall see it together."

This is our hope. This is the faith that I go back to the South with. With this faith we will be able to hew out of the mountain of despair a stone of hope. With this faith we will be able to transform the jangling discords[4] of our nation into a beautiful symphony of brotherhood. With this faith we will be able to work together, to pray together, to struggle together, to stand up for freedom together, knowing that we will be free one day.

---

[1]a place offering relief as from difficulty
[2]to interrupt or come between
[3]to make valueless or useless
[4]disagreements

And this will be the day. This will be the day when all of God's children will be able to sing with new meaning "My country 'tis of thee, sweet land of liberty, of thee I sing. Land where my fathers died, land of the pilgrim's pride, from every mountainside, let freedom ring."

And if America is to be a great nation this must become true. So let freedom ring from the prodigious[5] hilltops of New Hampshire. Let freedom ring from the mighty mountains of New York. Let freedom ring from the heightening Alleghenies of Pennsylvania!

Let freedom ring from the snowcapped Rockies of Colorado!

Let freedom ring from the curvaceous slopes of California!

But not only that; let freedom ring from Stone Mountain of Georgia! Let freedom ring from Lookout Mountain of Tennessee.

Let freedom ring from every hill and molehill of Mississippi. From every mountainside, let freedom ring.

And when this happens, and when we allow freedom to ring, when we let it ring from every village and every hamlet, from every state and every city, we will be able to speed up that day when all of God's children, black men and white men, Jews and Gentiles, Protestants and Catholics, will be able to join hands and sing in the words of that old Negro spiritual, "Free at last! Free at last! Thank God almighty, we are free at last!"

---

[5]enormous; huge

REFLECT ····································

Which two readings tell of a loss of harmony with
nature, an end to living off the land?

What makes a good leader? Were Chief Black Hawk
and Martin Luther King, Jr., both good leaders? Give
a reason for your opinion.

Describe what you think life was like in Appalachia
in the early 1900s, given the absence of radios, TVs,
cars, railroads, and airplanes.

Which of these voices from the past did you find
most interesting? Why?

"Farewell to Black Hawk" is written by Black Hawk
in the first person, using "I" at the beginning, and
then changes to the third person, using "he." Why do
you think he wrote his speech this way?

How do you think Black Hawk and Everette Tharp
would feel about the environment today?

WRITE ·

Have you ever known an elderly person who talked about the past and the changes he or she has seen? Write a paragraph briefly describing the oral history you were told.

Write a short speech. Use the "I Have a Dream" speech as a model. List four or five of your hopes for the future. Begin each paragraph with "I have a dream that. . . ."

In 1963, Martin Luther King, Jr., hoped that all people in America would one day be treated equally. Do you think we are getting closer today to equality for all people? Write a few paragraphs supporting your opinion.

Imagine that you are a columnist. Choose one way you see our world changing (environment, laws and rules, car or house designs, fashions, lifestyles). Write a few paragraphs expressing your opinion for a column that might appear in your local newspaper.

The Watts Towers, created by Simon Rodia, rising from the Los Angeles landscape

REALIZING DREAMS

Do you believe that you have the ability to do anything you want to do in life?

Do you think that if you want something bad enough or work hard enough, anything can happen? Some people have a great desire to succeed and fulfill their dreams. Other people give up or do not think their dreams are realistic or possible.

Martin Luther King, Jr., said, "I have a dream." Although he died before those dreams came true, he lived with a purpose because of his dreams. You will read about three people who worked to make their dreams come true.

As you read, think about your dreams—ones you have had in the past and ones you still have now. What do you hope will happen to you and to the world during your lifetime?

Robert Fulghum said, rather simply, that all of the important truths of life are learned by the time we are five. "Live a balanced life—learn some and think some and draw and paint and sing and dance and work every day some. . . . Be aware of wonder. . . . Imagination is stronger than knowledge. . . . Hope always triumphs over experience. . . . Dreams are more powerful than facts."

In this reading, Robert Fulghum tells about a "dreamer"—a man who wanted to fly and look down on the world from the clouds. We often say that people with unusual goals "have their heads in the clouds." Larry Walters does.

Larry Walters

From *All I Really Need to Know I Learned in Kindergarten*
Robert Fulghum

Now let me tell you about Larry Walters, my hero. Walters is a truck driver, thirty-three years old. He is sitting in his lawn chair in his backyard, wishing he could fly. For as long as he could remember, he wanted to go *up*. To be able to just rise right up in the air and see for a long way. The time, money, education, and opportunity to be a pilot were not his. Hang gliding[1] was too dangerous, and any good place for gliding was too far away. So he spent a lot of summer after-

---

[1]sport of riding a device like a large kite or wing

noons sitting in his backyard in his ordinary old aluminum lawn chair—the kind with the webbing and rivets. Just like the one you've got in your backyard.

The next chapter in this story is carried by the newspapers and television. There's old Larry Walters up in the air over Los Angeles. Flying at last. Really getting UP there. Still sitting in his aluminum lawn chair, but it's hooked on to forty-five helium-filled surplus weather balloons. Larry has a parachute on, a CB radio, a six-pack of beer, some peanut butter and jelly sandwiches, and a BB gun to pop some of the balloons to come down. And instead of being just a couple of hundred feet over his neighborhood, he shot up eleven thousand feet, right through the approach corridor to the Los Angeles International Airport.

Walters is a taciturn[2] man. When asked by the press why he did it, he said: "You can't just sit there." When asked if he was scared, he answered: "Wonderfully so." When asked if he would do it again, he said: "Nope." And asked if he was glad that he did it, he grinned from ear to ear and said: "Oh, yes."

The human race sits in its chair. On the one hand is the message that says there's nothing left to do. And the Larry Walterses of the earth are busy tying balloons to their chairs, directed by dreams and imagination to do their thing.

The human race sits in its chair. On the one hand is the message that the human situation is hopeless. And the Larry Walterses of the earth soar upward knowing anything is possible, sending back the message from eleven thousand feet: "I did it, I really did it. I'm FLYING!"

It's the spirit here that counts. The time may be long, the vehicle may be strange or unexpected. But if

---

[2]quiet; not talkative

the dream is held close to the heart, and imagination is applied to what there is close at hand, everything is still possible.

But wait! Some cynic[3] from the edge of the crowd insists that human beings still *can't really* fly. Not like birds, anyway. True. But somewhere in some little garage, some maniac[4] with a gleam in his eye is scarfing[5] vitamins and mineral supplements, and practicing flapping his arms faster and faster.

---

[3]a person who doubts the goodness or sincerity of others
[4]insane person; lunatic
[5]eating greedily

In a book, an author sometimes adds a postscript to tell what happened after the book was written. Beautiful Junk *is a story about Charlie, a boy who discovers an old man filling a wheelbarrow with junk. The old man collects pieces of tile, metal, bottle, glass, shells, and other objects from garbage cans every day. Charlie follows the man and finds out that he is building some beautiful towers.*

This postscript tells the true story about how the towers were built in the Watts section of Los Angeles, California, by Simon Rodia.

Postscript

From *Beautiful Junk*
Jon Madian

Simon Rodia was a poor man who worked as a tile setter. He liked to read about heroes like Marco Polo, Columbus, and Galileo. Once he said that a person has to do "good good or bad bad to be remembered." Maybe it was because Simon Rodia wanted to be remembered for doing something very good that he worked for thirty-three years to build the towers.

Simon Rodia worked all alone. He used only the simple tools of a tile setter and a window washer's belt and bucket. For building materials, he collected more than seventy-thousand seashells, dismantled pipe structures and steel bedframes, and salvaged countless tiles and bottles.

In 1954, at the age of seventy-five, Simon Rodia

completed his work, and he moved away. Many people thought he was a crazy man for building the towers. Children broke the tile and glass decorations. In 1957, Simon Rodia's house burned down. It seemed that his work was going to be destroyed and forgotten.

Some people realized how wonderful the towers were and wanted to save them. But the Los Angeles City Building Department said that the towers must be destroyed because they were unsafe, having been built from junk and with inferior construction methods.

A missile test engineer, using space-age calculations, showed that though Simon Rodia had little book knowledge of the right way to build, his construction was safe. The building officials still were not satisfied. A pull test of the tallest tower was ordered. A cable was hooked from a truck to the top of the tallest tower. While television cameras turned and hundreds of people watched, the truck strained to pull the tower down. A shout of joy went up from the crowd. The tower stood firm. Only one seashell had fallen out of place.

Today people come from all over the world to enjoy Simon Rodia's towers. Pictures of the towers appear in magazines from Tokyo to Paris. Simon Rodia's dream has come true. He is remembered for something beautiful.

The speaker, a Mexican-American woman, is Vice President of U.S. WEST Communications. This speech was written and delivered for women attending a conference called "Adelante Mujer" (On-ward Women) on May 19, 1990. She urges women to achieve their dreams.

It's Up to Us

Janice Payan

It's time for *Hispanic women* to believe we can get ahead, *because we can*. And because *we must*. Our families and workplaces and communities and nation need us to reach our full potential. There are jobs to be done, children to be raised, opportunities to be seized. We must look at those opportunities, choose the ones we will respond to, and *do something about them.*

We must do so, for others. And we must do so, for ourselves. *Yes*, there are barriers. You're up against racism, sexism, and too much month at the end of the money. *But so was any role model you choose.*

Look at Patricia Diaz-Denis. Patricia was one of nine or ten children in a Mexican-American family that had low means, but high hopes. Her parents said Patricia should go to college. But they had no money. So, little by little, Patricia scraped up the money to send herself.

Her boyfriend was going to be a lawyer. And he told Patricia, "You should be a lawyer, too, because *nobody can argue like you do!*" Well, Patricia didn't even know what a lawyer was, but she became one—so successful that she eventually was appointed to the

Federal Communications Commission in Washington, D.C.

Or look at Toni Panteha, a Puerto Rican who grew up in a shack with dirt floors, no father, and often no food. But through looking and listening, she realized the power of *community*—the fact that people with very little, when working together, can create much.

Dr. Panteha has created several successful institutions in Puerto Rico, and to me, *she* is an institution. I can see the wisdom in her eyes, hear it in her voice, wisdom far beyond herself, like Mother Teresa.

Or look at Ada Kirby, a Cuban girl whose parents put her on a boat for Miami. Mom and Dad were to follow on the next boat, but they never arrived. So Ada grew up in an orphanage in Pueblo, and set some goals, and today is an executive director at U.S. WEST's research laboratories.

Each of these women was Hispanic, physically deprived, but *mentally awakened to the possibilities of building a better world*, both for others and for themselves.

Virtually every Hispanic woman in America started with a similar slate. In fact, let's do a quick survey. If you were born into a home whose economic status was something *less than rich* . . . please raise your hand.

It's a good thing I didn't ask the *rich* to raise their hands. I wouldn't have known if anyone was listening.

All right. So you were not born rich. As Patricia, Toni, and Ada have shown us, it doesn't matter. It's the choices we make from there on, that make the difference.

If you're thinking, "that's easy for *you* to say, Payan," then I'm thinking: "little do you know. . . ."

If you think I got where I am because I'm smarter than you, or have more energy than you, you're wrong.

If I'm so smart, why can't I parallel park?

If I'm so energetic, why do I still need eight hours of sleep a night? And I mean *need*. If I hadn't had my eight hours last night, you wouldn't even want to *hear* what I'd be saying this morning!

I am more like you and you are more like me than you would guess.

I'm a third-generation Mexican-American . . . born into a lower middle-class family right here in Denver. My parents married young; she was pregnant. My father worked only about half the time during my growing-up years. He was short on education, skills, and confidence. There were drug and alcohol problems in the family. My parents finally sent my older brother to a Catholic high school, in hopes that would help him. They sent me to the same school, to *watch* him. That was okay.

In public school I never could choose between the "Greasers" and the "Soshes." I wanted desperately to feel that I "belonged." *But I did not like feeling that I had to deny my past to have a future.*

Anybody here ever feel that way?

Anyway, the more troubles my brother had, the more I vowed to avoid them. So, in a way, he was my inspiration. As Victor Frankl says, there is meaning in every life.

By the way, that brother later died after returning from Vietnam.

I was raised with typical Hispanic female expectations. In other words: If you want to *do* well in life, you'd better . . . can anybody finish that sentence?

Right! *Marry well.*

I liked the idea of loving and marrying someone, but I felt like he should be more than a "meal ticket." And I felt like *I* should be more than a leech. I didn't want to feel so dependent.

So I set my goals on having a marriage, a family, *and* a career. I didn't talk too much about those goals, so nobody told me they bordered on *insanity* for a Hispanic woman in the 1960s.

At one point, I even planned to become a doctor. But Mom and Dad said "wait a minute. That takes something like 12 years of college."

I had no idea how I was going to pay for *four* years of college, let alone *12.* But what scared me more than the cost was the *time:* In 12 years I'd be an *old woman.*

Time certainly changes your perspective on that.

My advice to you is, if you want to be a doctor, go for it! It doesn't take 12 years, anyway.

If your dreams include a career that requires college . . . go for it!

You may be several years older when you finish, but by that time you'd be several years older if you *don't* finish college, too.

For all my suffering in high school, I finished near the top of my graduating class. I dreamed of attending the University of Colorado, at Boulder. You want to know what my counselor said? You already know. That I should go to a business college for secretaries, at most.

But I went to the University of Colorado, anyway. I arranged my own financial aid: a small grant, a low paying job, and a *big* loan.

I just thank God that this was the era when jeans and sweatshirts were getting popular. That was all I had!

I'm going to spare you any description of my class work, except to say that it was difficult—and worth every painful minute. . . .

REFLECT ·

Robert Fulghum writes, "The human race sits in its chair." What should we be doing instead?

Which type of person are you, a doubter or a dreamer? Are you content to sit in a chair, or would you rather try to fly in it?

How are Simon Rodia and Larry Walters alike?

According to Janice Payan, what barriers do Hispanic women face?

Janice Payan is now a successful executive and is living her dream. What was the most important step toward realizing her achievements?

WRITE ·

Choose one of the three people and write a letter telling why you admire him or her.

Simon Rodia wanted to be remembered for doing something good. What do you want people to remember about you?

"The sky's the limit." If you had no limitations (education, money, or family obligations), what would your dream be? If you could do anything you wanted to do, what would it be?

A woman searching the Vietnam War Memorial for the name of a lost loved one

LETTERS AND VERSES ABOUT WAR

Have you ever been away from loved ones? Did you miss family and friends? How did you cope?

When soldiers go off to war, they must adjust quickly. They are far from home and all that is familiar to them, and they are facing danger and possible death. Their families at home must also adjust to missing their loved ones who have been sent away to fight in a war.

The following selections are letters and verses sent to and from the battlefront. The wars are the American Civil War (1860s), the Vietnam War (1960s–1970s), and the Persian Gulf War—"Operation Desert Storm" (1991). The first two writers are soldiers who write home about their experiences. The third writer is a husband who sends love poems to his wife while she is serving in the war.

As you read, think about who and what you would miss most if you were separated from loved ones.

The Civil War began in April 1861. Confederate and Union forces fought in a battle near the town of Manassas by a creek called Bull Run.

A week before the battle, Major Sullivan Ballou of the 2nd Rhode Island wrote home to his wife in Smithfield.

Letter from Major Sullivan Ballou

From *The Civil War: An Illustrated History*
Geoffrey C. Ward, Ric Burns, and Ken Burns

July 14, 1861
Camp Clark, Washington

My very dear Sarah:

The indications are very strong that we shall move in a few days—perhaps tomorrow. Lest I should not be able to write again, I feel impelled to write a few lines that may fall under your eye when I shall be no more. . . .

I have no misgivings about, or lack of confidence in the cause in which I am engaged, and my courage does not halt or falter. I know how strongly American Civilization now leans on the triumph of the Government, and how great a debt we owe to those who went before us through the blood and sufferings of the Revolution. And I am willing—perfectly willing—to lay down all my joys in this life, to help maintain this Government, and to pay that debt. . . .

Sarah my love for you is deathless, it seems to bind me with mighty cables that nothing but Omnipotence[1] could break; and yet my love of Country comes

---

[1]Divine power; name for God

over me like a strong wind and bears me unresistibly on with all these chains to the battle field.

The memories of the blissful moments I have spent with you come creeping over me, and I feel most gratified to God and to you that I have enjoyed them so long. And hard it is for me to give them up and burn to ashes the hopes of future years, when, God willing, we might still have lived and loved together, and seen our sons grown up to honorable manhood, around us. I have, I know, but few and small claims upon Divine Providence, but something whispers to me—perhaps it is the wafted[2] prayer of my little Edgar, that I shall return to my loved ones unharmed. If I do not my dear Sarah, never forget how much I love you, and when my last breath escapes me on the battle field, it will whisper your name. Forgive my many faults, and the many pains I have caused you. How thoughtless and foolish I have often times been! How gladly would I wash out with my tears every little spot upon your happiness. . . .

But, O Sarah! if the dead can come back to this earth and flit unseen around those they loved, I shall always be near you; in the gladdest days and in the darkest nights . . . *always, always,* and if there be a soft breeze upon your cheek, it shall be my breath, as the cool air fans your throbbing temple, it shall be my spirit passing by. Sarah do not mourn me dead; think I am gone and wait for thee, for we shall meet again. . . .

Sullivan Ballou was killed at the first battle of Bull Run [on July 21, 1861].

---

[2]carried along; transported

The writer of this letter was stationed in Vietnam. During the late 1960s the number of deaths from the Vietnamese war was high. Americans at home were debating our involvement in the war. When the soldiers came home, they were not greeted by parades, but by thousands of angry people who wanted peace at home and our troops out of Vietnam.

This letter was sent home to family members. It is filled with details of the long days spent in a jungle climate—far from home in Ohio.

Letter from 1Lt. Sharon A. Lane

From *Dear America: Letters Home from Vietnam*
Edited by Bernard Edelman

4 June 1969
Wednesday

Dear Mom & Dad,

Got your letter of 28th, Mom, yesterday, 3 June. Today I got Dad's of 26th April. Never know what is going on with the mail. Haven't gotten the package yet. Heaven only knows when they will arrive and in what condition.

Worked in ICU [Intensive Care Unit] again today. Was lucky, got to 102° today, and ICU is air-conditioned. They have a lot of really sick patients. Had three die yesterday. They still have four on respirators. None too good, either.

One of the GI's who died yesterday was from Ward 8, medical. Had malaria. During the previous night he had been nauseated and kept getting up to the latrine[1] to vomit. Got up at 2 A.M. and was running to the latrine. Fell really hard and cracked his head on the cement floor. The nurse who was on duty said you could *hear* his skull fracture. He immediately started bleeding from ears and nose and stopped breathing. Then had cardiac arrest. They got him going again and transferred him to ICU but he died anyway yesterday. Had severe brain damage. Other death was [a] GI with multiple fragment wounds from a mine explosion. He was there two weeks ago when I worked that other day in ICU. Also a Vietnamese died. Don't know what was wrong with him.

Census hit the 10,000 mark yesterday. This unit, the 312th [Evacuation Hospital], has treated 10,000 patients since [we] arrived last September. Unbelievable. Registrar office had a poll going as to what time and what date the 10,000th patient would be admitted. Was yesterday morning. Haven't heard who won the money yet.

They put plastic or rubber? floor tile down in the mess hall the evening before last. Looked real nice until yesterday noon when it got hot. The tar came up between the tile and it got tracked all over the place. Couldn't move your chair at all. It was stuck to the floor.

How did the home-made ice cream turn out? Start "nights" tomorrow so don't have to get up early tomorrow. Nice thought.

Still very quiet around here. Haven't gotten mortared[2] for couple of weeks now. We are getting some new nurses this week. They are from the unit who will take over when the 312th goes home in September. Their hospital is farther south somewhere. They are

---

[1]washroom
[2]shelled, fired on

handling 80% Vietnamese casualties now so are turning their hospital over to the Viets and coming here to take over. Supposed to get the new chief nurse tomorrow. So the unit will change names in September. However, they are supposed to be an RA [Regular Army] group. Not a reserve unit like the 312th is. Things are supposed to get a lot more "strict Army style." No one is looking forward to it.

Read a book last night and missed a good Lee Marvin movie at the mess hall.

Had a movie star visit here the second or third week I was here. Named Ricardo Montalban? Ever hear of him? Forgot to mention it previously. Some of the older people here remembered him. Said he was in movies with Esther Williams.

Will stop for now. Getting sleepy.

See you sooner.

Shar

1Lt. Sharon A. Lane, a nurse from Canton, Ohio, arrived at the 312th Evacuation Hospital, Chu Lai, in April 1969. Two months later, on 8 June, she was killed by shrapnel during a rocket attack. She was one month short of her 26th birthday.

In January 1991, American soldiers joined forces with other countries against the country of Iraq. Under dictator Saddam Hussein, Iraqi soldiers had illegally taken over the country of Kuwait.

What followed was Operation Desert Storm, a short war that was fought with high-tech missiles and weapons. The United States and its allies easily defeated Hussein's army. During each day of the war, however, families of American soldiers feared for the lives of their loved ones serving in the war. Friends and strangers sent letters and cards to support the soldiers.

This reading includes poetry written by George Albertini, Jr., to his wife, an army officer stationed in Saudi Arabia. He wanted to show his love and support while she was serving far from home.

Poetry and War

From *Desert Warriors*
The Staff of *USA Today*

Valentine's Day is approaching, and Capt. Michelle Perna is stationed in Saudi Arabia, far from those she loves. Her husband, George Albertini, Jr., waits for her back in Washington, D.C., praying for her safety and writing love poems to her.

The poems "really help me get through all of this," says Perna, an Army transport officer with the 507th Support Group near the Kuwait border.

For Albertini, the verses he lovingly composes help ease the pain of their separation. "Of course, I wish she were back here, safe," says Albertini, who met Perna when he was a police lieutenant in Greenville, N.C., lecturing in one of her college classes. "But Michelle's very dedicated. She's very, very patriotic. One of her favorite scenes is the Statue of Liberty—that's her lady."

Albertini says his wife is in the Army "because she really believes in what she's doing. I knew from the beginning, when this all started, that she would want to go and be a part of it."

Before the Iraqi invasion of Kuwait, Perna, 24, had planned to shift from regular Army to reserve. Albertini, her husband of three years, had moved to Washington to work at her father's construction company. Before she joined her husband in the capital, however, she wanted her promotion to captain.

When her captain's bars came through last summer, she filed her resignation papers. Then what she calls "the Kuwait thing" blew up August 2.

"The only hesitation I have," says Albertini, "is I don't believe they [women] are getting enough credit for the work they do. As far as being able to do the job, I have no hesitation at all. My wife can outperform a lot of her male peers."

Until she returns, Perna will have to cling to Albertini's love verses. "He used to write poems when we first met," says Perna, "but he hadn't for a while. Now he's writing them again."

A selection of George Albertini's poetry, written for his Army wife, Capt. Michelle Perna:

Storm clouds are on the horizon
Watch for the moonless night
Gather together your words of death
And meet on the desert to fight.

The pace has quickened, adrenaline flows,
Now ready yourself for war
The eyes of the world are upon you
As destiny knocks at your door.

All that is right stands with you
In the test that is yet to come.
Remember we love you when days turn dark
And your spirit grows weary and numb.

We stand humbled by your sacrifice
As you enter the dark side of the sun.
Your purpose gives hope to all free people,
Your cause is a noble one.

So remember my love in the coming days
As you face this cold cruel test
Through the screaming hell of shot and shell
You are our country's best.

REFLECT·····································

Does each writer say how it feels to be in a war or to have a loved one in a war?

Which of the three writers has seen the most effects of war?

George Albertini, Jr., writes to his wife, "Your purpose gives hope to all free people, your cause is a noble one." Do you agree or disagree with this view of the Persian Gulf War? Explain.

Do you agree that you can say things in a letter that you cannot say in person? Why?

WRITE·····································

Have you ever been homesick? Write a journal entry for a date (day and year) when you missed your loved ones. Describe why you were away from home and how you felt.

"Going off to war" is not as glamorous as it may sound. Besides facing danger, soldiers must deal with being away from what is familiar to them. Write a few paragraphs describing what you would miss most if you were to go to war.

Write a letter using one of these points of view:

- from Mrs. Sullivan Ballou after getting her husband's letter
- to someone you need to say something to but cannot say in person
- to someone you've left behind as you've gone off to war

CREDITS